PRACTICAL WAYS
TO
PREVENT BURGLARY
AND
ILLEGAL ENTRY

BY

VAL MOOLMAN

GALAHAD BOOKS · NEW YORK CITY

Published by Galahad Books, a division of A & W Promo-
tional Book Corporation, 95 Madison Avenue, New York,
N.Y. 10016, by arrangement with Cornerstone Library

Library of Congress Catalog Card No.: 73-81632
ISBN: 0-88365-062-2

Manufactured in the United States of America.

DEDICATION

I wish to express my most heartfelt thanks to the many people and organizations who helped me so much in the research and preparation of this book, and my regrets for not being able to mention them all by name. There are too many of them—locksmiths, lock manufacturers, police officers, private investigators, security personnel, various law enforcement agencies and consumer-oriented service bureaus, automobile and auto parts dealers, representatives of burglar alarm companies, theft victims, and informants of one kind and another—for me to present a complete list. At the same time it would be unfair to pick out a few individual names for mention, since virtually all contributors—and they, at least, know who they are and how grateful I am to them—deserve equal thanks. Yet if I were to single out one person whose help was truly immeasurable, invaluable and essential, it would have to be locksmith Sal Schillizzi.

It was he who guided me along every step of the way and gave me the full benefit of his patience and professional expertise. The locksmithing world knows him well as a man with impeccable credentials: Active locksmith of long standing, ingenious inventor and holder of a number of patents, past president of the New York Locksmiths Association and now its Chairman of the Board, outstanding member of the Associated Locksmiths of America, president of the Insured Locksmiths and Safemen of America, Safecracking Champion of the World (in honest competition, that is), plain-spoken consultant to many lock manufacturers, expert witness on locks and safety devices before Senate subcommittees, legislative committees and grand juries, guest speaker on innumerable TV and radio shows—and instructor par excellence in the fine art of locking out burglars. It is to him, now my good friend, that I extend my warmest thanks, and to him—Sal Schillizzi, dedicated locksmith—that I dedicate this book.

TABLE OF CONTENTS

CONTENTS

CHAPTER ONE

WE ARE ALL VICTIMS

It is a hellishly hot day in the inner city, a day for air-conditioning and cold beer. There isn't much of either available for the people of this near-slum. But the man at the door of apartment 3D isn't thinking of cool air or beer. He is thinking of a desperately needed fix, and he is thinking of the money in the top drawer under the socks. It is his sister's apartment, and his brother-in-law's, but he no longer has a key. She refused him a key some time ago when she changed the lock. But she made a mistake, and he knows it. The cheap springlatch is a joke and the door frame is battered and warped.

His nailfile makes short work of the tapered latch. But— damn!—she's double-locked the door. There is a sound of a step downstairs and the sweat breaks out on his face. He must hurry. He wedges the screwdriver in between the door and the frame and levers it savagely. Door and frame inch apart. The bolt is free. He goes in swiftly, takes the money from under the socks, takes her few pathetic pieces of jewelry, takes the transistor radio, hears a step outside the door and runs to the window. It is held in place with a rubber-tipped wedge. He claws the wedge away, opens the window, and vaults out onto the fire escape. Well, so what if she is his own sister? If you can get it close to home and you've got to have it, why not? Anyway, she's always been a bitch.

* * * * *

There are few wealthy town houses left in our large eastern cities, but those that remain are attractive in a number of ways. Number one, they *are* wealthy; number two, their owners often have country homes or yachts or out-of-town interests that require their attention; number three, the homes are usually on quiet, secluded streets whose other inhabitants are of similar nature and tend to mind their own business.

One Thursday afternoon the owner's car draws away from the house on 72nd street and begins its weekly trip to the country home for the long weekend. The shades are pulled down, doors and windows are locked, and with the setting of the sun a photoelectrically-activated light is due to go on. It lights the inside of the house quite as if someone is at home.

The watchers on the corner see it go on. The same thing has been happening every weekend for many weeks. One of the young men strolls around to the rear of the house, takes a slim, curved metal piece from his pocket (he knows which one of his little tools will do the trick, because he inspected all the locks last weekend), and gently inserts it into the keyway. It takes him a moment or two, so that by the time he has the door open his friend has joined him . . . accompanied by two girls.

They have a lovely weekend. Late on Sunday night they bring their car to the neat little alleyway alongside the house and load it with silver, foodstuffs, liquor, clothing, furs, appliances from a miniature tape recorder to a color TV set, some currency, and a nice little pile of jewelry. Apart from this clearing operation, they do not bother to clean up behind them. Dirty dishes, broken glasses, overflowing ashtrays, disheveled beds and general chaos lie in their wake. Has anybody noticed their presence? Not a soul. Even the lights they burned at night behind the drawn shades have been camouflaged by the burglar-chasing light that goes on every evening at sundown and off again with the coming of dawn.

* * * * *

It is a bright spring day in a placid section of Queens. The block is a "nice" one, part business and part residential. There are a few multiple-family dwellings (for six to eight families), eleven small stores, a beauty parlor, a TV repair shop, and a couple of one-story homes. In the basement of one of them lies the body of a housewife. She has been raped, stabbed and strangled, and her pocketbook is missing. Her front door is unlocked. It is equipped with neither chain nor peephole.

Her neighbors, attracted by the arrival of the police, stand in horrified clusters on the sidewalk. Shock is mixed with incredulity. "Here, on our own street!" one housewife exclaims, and shakes her head. "It's reached us now. What are we going to do—bolt ourselves into our houses, make our homes into jails? My God, this kind of thing never used to happen here!"

A storekeeper shakes his head. "Maybe not this kind of thing. But with the stores it's been bad. Lately it's been real bad. I've been hit five times in the last eighteen months."

* * * * *

It is a cold, dark January night in the comfortable little Pennsylvania town. At the far end of the driveway is a friendly house in the trees, light and laughter spilling from it. At the street end of the driveway it is dark; there are no street lights in the immediate area. Cars fill the driveway, and more cars line the curb. The one last in line is a late model semi-luxury car in good condition.

A man strolls down the street and stops beside it. He is a youngish man, quite well-dressed. His appearance suggests that he might very well be the owner of a fine car himself. He is not, however, the owner of this particular car, although he does know a likely buyer. He gives the car a fast once-over for any sign of alarm or tricky locking device, finds none, then tries the doors and gives a quiet grunt of satisfaction. One of the rear doors is unlocked. That saves him a few seconds, anyway. Before those few seconds have passed he is driving through the darkness to a place where he will stop and change the plates, after which he will make another very short trip to a workshop where a few more changes will be made and he will collect his money.

The Soaring Cost of Crime

It is happening every day throughout the United States. That crime rates are soaring we all know, but it may not be generally realized that crimes against property currently make up 87 percent of the Crime Index offenses reported by the F.B.I.

Burglary, which may be defined as "the unlawful entry or attempted unlawful entry of a structure to commit a felony or theft, even though no force is used to gain entrance," heads the list on the F.B.I.'s SCALE OF MAJOR CRIMES. That is to say, it occurs more often than any other crime: In 1968, *every 17 seconds* saw another burglary committed in our land. The first six months of 1969 showed a 3 percent rise over the corresponding period in 1968.

Let's take a look at the annual rise of the burglary rate, in terms of loss to ourselves. In 1966, burglary cost Americans $284 million. In 1967, 1,600,000 homes (including apartments) were invaded by burglars, to the tune of $350 million. In 1968 there were 1,828,900 burglaries, with a dollar loss to property owners of $545 million. 1969? Time will tell; but when the figures are toted up, they will be astronomical.

In New York alone there are more than 15,000 burglaries a month. On Manhattan's luxurious East Side there are reportedly 1,000 ourglaries a month. No one really knows how many *unreported* burglaries there are in less elegant areas. The relatives of thieving addicts do not always make reports. Many small storekeepers throughout the land, repeatedly hit, fail to report all losses. The poor, and members of minority groups, do not always take their troubles to the police. Affluent parents of delinquents have been known to make unofficial restitution. It is possible that there are as many unreported burglaries as those that hit the record books.

The figures on reported crimes indicate that the householder, including the apartment dweller, gets the worst of it. Of the dollar losses suffered in 1968, residential burglary losses amounted to $311 million and nonresidential burglary losses amounted to $234 million. In that period, residential burglary accounted for 54 percent of the total, with nonresidential burglary accounting for the remaining 46 percent.

Even more alarming than the dollar loss is the rising incidence of the crime and the increasing boldness of the criminals. We see a pattern emerging when we take a look at the burglary figures for the period 1960-1968: During that time, nonresidential nighttime burglary rose 57 percent, while nonresidential *daytime* burglary rose 124 percent. And during that time, residential nighttime burglary rose 91 percent, while residential *daytime* burglary rose 247 percent. The only thing that declined was the average age of the offenders. In 1968, 55 percent of those arrested for burglary were less than 18 years old.

The facts on auto theft are just as dismal. Automobile theft rates appear to be going up by more than 100,000 per year. Approximately 550,000 cars were stolen in 1966. 654,900 auto thefts were recorded for 1967. 777,800 motor vehicles were reported stolen in 1968. Estimates indicate that auto thefts per year will have climbed to the 900,000 mark by the time the 1969 figures are tabulated, and to 1,000,000 or more by the end of 1970. The theft rate rose 129 percent over the years 1960-1968, and in the first six months of 1969 it rose 9 percent over the same period of the previous year.

Eyebrow-raising figures? Or merely tedious statistics? Well, figures may not be very exciting, but we should manage to raise an eyebrow when we consider the following: Regularly, over the past several years, eight out of every ten stolen cars had been left unlocked by the owners prior to the theft. Four out of ten were taken with the ignition left unlocked by the owner or with the key actually in the ignition. Others presented almost equal opportunities and were easily compromised. Who took them? For the most part, nonprofessionals. Opportunists. It scarcely takes a professional thief to pull off an auto theft under these conditions. In fact, 79-80 percent of all car thieves arrested are under the age of 21. Brace yourself for some more statistics and think of your own children: In 1968, 61 percent of all persons arrested for the crime of auto theft were under eighteen years of age, and 16 percent had not yet reached the tender age of fifteen. Of all the F.B.I.'s Crime Index offenses, auto theft has by far the largest proportion of arrests of people under the age of 18. Few of these youngsters are hardened criminals; few are technically capable of taking a locked car.

The above figures are, like most figures, subject to manipulation. The "persons arrested" for auto theft are not necessarily typical of the auto thief. Although about 86 percent of all stolen vehicles are recovered, only 19 percent of the thefts are solved by the arrest of the offender. There can be no doubt that the highly skilled, well-organized professional is less likely to be caught than the fumbling amateur, and that the profile of the offender obtained from the arrest records may be very misleading. Nevertheless, the twin facts remain: It is too easy to steal automobiles, and our own youngsters are doing much of the stealing.

Thus the personal cost to Americans is high. So is the dollar loss. The 14 percent of vehicles that are unrecovered represent an annual loss to the victims of well over $100 million dollars. True, 55 percent of stolen vehicles are recovered within 48 hours—but in what condition!

Public Protection and Private Attitudes

We spend a great deal of time complaining about our various state and local law enforcement agencies and doing relatively little to support them. There is some genuine cause for complaint, but what we cannot blame on our police forces is the rising crime rate. In 1968 there were close to 4.5 million major crimes recorded in the United States—approximately one crime for every 45 citizens. During that same period our cities were under the protection of 240,275 full-time police department employees, including civilians—an average of 2.1 police employees per 1000 inhabitants. Obviously, not all of these employees are on duty during any single 8-hour shift. The wonder is not that there is so much crime, reported or otherwise, but that there isn't very much more . . . particularly since we do so little to protect ourselves.

Private security agencies play some part in the protection of homeowners and businessmen. Their limitations are not the subject of this book but, largely because of their private status, they clearly *do* have limitations. Certainly they cannot fully compensate for shorthanded police forces, public apathy and private carelessness.

Not that the public is always apathetic. People are becoming afraid. A recent survey came up with the conclusion that one-third of the American people feel safe at night in their own neighborhoods and in their own houses. Twenty percent are so fearful that they would, if they could, move out of their neighborhoods to what they think are safer areas. These people would probably be even more unnerved to learn that there is hardly any such thing as a "safe" area. Of that, more later—but in the meantime what we should be doing is thinking of our self-protection instead of wallowing in our fears and making wild outcries about law, order, and try-to-find-a-cop-when-you-need-one!

We seem to be generally unaware of the fact that both burglary and auto theft are essentially crimes of opportunity, very frequently committed under conditions provided for the thief by the victim himself. In our ignorance we are almost united. In our attitudes toward the problem we are not. Digging into attitudes, we find roughly five types, or schools of thought:

1. *God help us.* These are the people who run scared. They huddle in their homes, afraid to be there and afraid to go out. They bar their windows, bolt their doors, and tremble. Some of these people spend a great deal of money (often too much) on elaborate security devices. Others, oddly enough, equip their doors and windows with masses of dime-store hardware and are astonished when it doesn't hold up against the ravages of time or forcible entry.

2. *It Can't Happen Here.* On the other end of the scale are the vast numbers of people who do practically nothing whatever to protect themselves and assume that whatever happens in this life (so long as it is unpleasant) will happen to somebody else. They may have either good or flimsy locks; they may or may not use them. These folks tend to live in the nice, middling-wealthy suburb where people go around saying, "Sure, the crime rate's going up, but so far—thank heaven!—nothing's happened here and I just

don't believe it's ever going to." And then they tell you proudly that they haven't locked their front door since they moved in umpteen years ago, except for their annual trip to Florida or Fire Island. They refuse to consider the fact that even a trip to the supermarket, leaving an unlocked house behind them, is a dangerously careless act. They are just as careless with their cars. Burglars and auto thieves just love them.

3. *Once Bitten, Twice Shy.* In this group we meet people who have been burglarized because of their own careless-ness. An unlocked door, an unguarded or open window, or an inferior lock has left them at the mercy of a thief. The house has been cleaned out. Too much! This must never happen again! Off they rush to the nearest locksmith and come home with armloads of expensive, and often largely superfluous and inappropriate, hardware with which to se-cure the shattered stable door. Overnight, the place turns into Leavenworth or the now-legendary Alcatraz. Up go the barricades, up goes the drawbridge, and out of that (locked?) window goes all sense of perspective.

4. *Oh, Hell, What's the Use?* Here we have the eternal pessimists. Their theory of existence is one of the abandon-ment of all hope and effort, and their proposition to themselves and others reads: "Why bother? If they want to get in, they'll get in." It goes further: "What do I want, my windows broken, my front door ruined? I should lock the car, and have them damage it getting in? No, sir, no matter what you do, they're going to get in, and why should they ruin my property while they're doing it?" When they are victimized they tend to yell bloody murder at the inefficiency of the police, tell everyone within earshot that they told you so, and take no blame whatsoever for not using the locks and alarms so readily available to them. Certainly they give no thought to the possibility that they may have encouraged a first offender, possibly a youngster, to take the first step in a life of crime by leaving their property temptingly un-guarded.

5. *Lightning Doesn't Strike Twice.* Right about here we encounter a group of people who have been burglarized once and now congratulate themselves that the laws of chance will protect them from further such encroachments. In their innocence they make little or no attempt to secure themselves against further intrusions. Either they have not heard of the Principle of the Returnee, or they regard it as a

tired old myth. In this they are wrong. It may be rare for lightning to strike twice in the same place, but it is not rare for burglary to strike twice at the same premises. The second burglary may be effected coincidentally; or it may be effected by an individual who has heard that this particular place is a soft touch; or it may be effected by the original burglar who, like so many fictional criminals and so many real-life criminals, "returns to the scene of the crime." A burglar will quite often return to the scene. Psychologists, police experts among them, claim that he does this out of an unconscious desire to get caught. He may return again and again until he has achieved his hidden desire. This is particularly true of the nonprofessional burglar, but it is often true of the professional as well. He will deny it, of course, but in many cases the hidden motivation is there.

You are sceptical? Beware. He *may* be back. And if he does come back, you had better have some well-chosen security hardware waiting for him, or he'll get in a second time.

Of course, there are variations on the above themes, and there are even people who do maintain a sense of proportion and who do take adequate protective measures. These are the people who are aware that the vast majority of entries are made into premises that are not equipped with the pick-resistant and jimmy-proof locks available today, or not even secured with the deadbolt feature that is common on so many of today's locks. They know, too, that the unlocked home or car is particularly vulnerable, and they use their locks and alarms.

It is perfectly true that there is no such thing as a totally burglar-proof installation. Given enough incentive (a dwelling known to be loaded with valuables) the skilled and well-organized burglar will be able to enter his target area *if* he is thoroughly prepared, has the appropriate knowledge and equipment, is allowed enough time, and is able to use possibly noisy tools without disturbing the neighbors. The insurance companies are well aware of this, and either charge accordingly or simply refuse coverage in certain areas or under certain conditions. "It's difficult to get coverage for theft and burglary where the householder is a person who is out at business all day and leaves his apartment empty," we are told by the Insurance Information Institute. What the insurance companies like to see is a house, apartment or store that is connected to a central alarm system which rings in the nearest police station or first-class protective agency.

Such protection costs the kind of money that we cannot all afford. Yet the determined and even skilled burglar can be delayed, often with disastrous consequences to himself, by sturdy locks of appropriate type efficiently installed . . . and used. He delights in the easily foiled snaplatch, but he dislikes the long bolt and the key-locked window. He fears noise, he fears any security device that consumes time and delays his entry. He particularly loathes the loud sound of an alarm siren alerting the neighbors while he is hacking away at a door equipped with a double-cylinder lock and a vertical deadbolt. He tends to want to run. Under these circumstances he can scarcely be expected to do his best work.

Burglars avoid the difficult, look for the easy. Your job: Make *his* job difficult. Locks and alarms that take time and tools to circumvent are, if not absolute protection, major *deterrents*. Light, illuminating his night work, is another. These deterrents must be used. They need not be costly to be effecttive.

It Pays to be Poor? There is a rumor abroad that the rich are robbed more often than the poor, and that the wealthier the neighborhood the more theft-prone it is. But try to tell that to the people in the ghettoes, in the slums, in the dock areas, in the struggling fringes of our cities. "A professional burglar who goes out to rob an apartment in a good area knows he's likely to come back with an armful of goodies," the New York Post of July 23, 1969 quotes an Aetna Insurance Company manager as saying. "He can't be. so sure if he tries a poorer neighborhood." Well, naturally. But what if circumstances restrict his activities to the poorer neighborhoods? What if he isn't "professional" enough to aim for high stakes? What if he's not looking for an armful of goodies, but one good shot in the arm—or even a square meal? How many "good areas" are there in our affluent land, compared with those that may be otherwise classified?

Many kinds of people and many degrees of skill are found in the ranks of those who make burglary their full-time or occasional profession. A very small minority are slick society thieves. Most of the others are not even truly professional in terms of know-how, training, and technique, although nearly all possess some degree of rudimentary skill. Many of them will steal from their friends and their mothers and their brothers, few of whom are likely to live in the better neighborhoods.

Really big hauls are comparatively rare. Of course it's going to hit the newspapers when 8 or 10 apartments in one building are burglarized in a single day or night. Of course the $50-100,000 jewel heist makes a bigger splash than the $5-10 pilfer from the Harlem housewife. It's more exciting copy—who cares to read about the 5-buck losses when Bill the Shill makes off with the movie siren's rubies?

Only the victims care. Maybe the papers run a few lines about the little burglaries; maybe they don't. Public outcries are not raised when appliances and little sums of cash are taken from the homes in lower-income projects. We hear about it when there is a wave of burglary in one of those "nice" suburbs, but we hear little about the thousands and thousands of less newsworthy cases in which the corner grocery store is broken into, the local drugstore opens in the morning to reveal empty shelves in the prescription department, the liquor store is held up, the neighborhood supermarket cleaned out, the insurance salesman's car is stolen. . . . Nor do we hear much, if anything, about the very ordinary people in very ordinary homes in city, suburb or small town throughout the country who come home from work or from vacations to find their very ordinary but nevertheless prized possessions gone. And we give very little thought to how the crime rate affects the people of the blighted neighborhoods, the ghetto areas, the cities' backyards and the wrong side of the tracks. In those places there are so many addicts and so many debt-ridden or plain hungry people breaking into each other's homes, or wandering a few blocks away from home to the nearest of the more affluent-looking houses, that nobody even keeps much track any more.

But the poor are not safe from burglary, any more than the rich, and in a way they have even more to lose.

Nationwide burglary figures, expressed in terms of number of offenses per 100,000 people in particular types of localities, reflect the popular assumption that burglary rates are highest in major cities, lower in smaller cities, lower yet in suburban areas, and lowest in rural areas. But before we start a stampede to what seems to be the comparative safety of the suburbs or the country, let us take a quick look at the percentages. True, in the big cities burglary rose by 12 percent in 1968 over 1967, and we can predict a comparable rise in the years to come. But it is also true that in the same period the suburban areas showed a 14 percent rise, while the rural areas began to creep up on the cities' rising burglary rate with an increase of 11 percent.

Rich, poor, or somewhere in between; city-dweller, villager, suburbanite or farmer; we are all victims. The crime of burglary is widespread throughout the land. Its potential reach is into every home (and even business) in this country: the small apartment building, the giant housing project, the duplex, the studio apartment, the house on a friendly tree-lined street, the rooms above a store, the lonely farmhouse, the slum shack and the mansion. The target area and the method chosen depend on the preferences and capabilities of the thief himself. Opportunity may give the burglar his biggest break; but how he uses that opportunity is up to him.

What is he like, this thief?

CHAPTER TWO

WANTED!

The Nature of The Beast

It may not be quite fair to call the man a "beast," for he ordinarily avoids violence and prefers to go unarmed. Once upon a time—not too many years ago—burglary was considered one of the more "honorable" of the criminal professions, and one still meets police officers who say that many of the burglars they pick up are "quite nice fellows." But times are changing, and the dividing line between burglary and more serious crimes is growing dimmer.

There are essentially two kinds of burglars, with subgroups in each category.

The first kind is the highly skilled professional pickman who spends time surveying his target, planning his campaign and arranging disposal of the goods. He works swiftly and neatly, leaves no damaging signs of his visit on locks, doors or windows, is very rarely armed, avoids violence at practically all costs, and usually steals only money and jewelry. At his best, he has brains, capital, a fast-moving car and maybe even an airline ticket to hasten his getaway. Sometimes he flies from his own home town to make a quick strike at an exclusive Park Avenue apartment, a wealthy home in Beverly Hills or an expensive hotel in Miami Beach, and flies back when his work is done. He may take back with him something like $60,000 or $100,000. Fortunately, he is a rare bird. His type may constitute only about one-half of one percent of the burgling fraternity.

Slightly more common is the professional of less finesse, a man who knows how to pick locks but lacks the suavity and resources of his superior in crime. He makes his living off the fairly nice homes and apartments of urban and suburban areas—and quite a good living it can be, because he, too, makes his plans with care, enters surreptitiously, and concentrates on jewelry and cash.

Time was when this breed of thief, the skilled pickman, was a relatively uncommon type: an outwardly urbane and at least semi-educated individual who could melt into quite elegant neighborhoods without being noticed and couldn't be bothered with the less affluent areas. Within the last few years, however, the ranks of pickmen have suddenly swelled to include some much less polished individuals who do not run true to type. They blend unobtrusively into the background of the poorer, rougher neighborhoods, the projects, the lower-to-middle class residential areas and the quietly decaying segments of cities of all sizes. These men have learned, one way or another, how to circumvent most standard locks and cylinders without the use of force.

Pickmen are still in the small minority among burglars. But in an alarming number of cases recently investigated in our major cities, it has been evident that some sort of picking device has been used. Devices employed may be one of several well-made sets used by locksmiths, and illegally acquired or copied; or they may be homemade. Bent wire, in the hands of a skilled professional, may be as effective as a genuine lockpick and almost as easy to use as a key. (Locksmith Sal Schillizzi, fortunately legitimate, can do wonders with a pair of bent bobby pins in a pin tumbler lock. It takes him a little longer than his commercially manufactured locksmith's pick, but not much. The extra time, he says, is spent on twisting the bobby pins into shape.) Depending on the quality of the lock cylinder, picking takes a little skill and time or a great deal of skill and time.

Of the dozens and dozens of locks on the market, most are capable of being picked or manipulated by a skilled pickman. Some, however, take hours to defeat. It is these pick-resistant locks that are the despair of the most practiced professional.

Even more frustrating for the skilled pickman are the truly pick-proof locks. The police hesitate to use the term "pick-proof," because the future may prove that these locks can eventually be picked by super-thieves. But, as of publication date, there are two fully pick-proof locks on the market; no one has yet been known to pick them. In fact, there is a third lock that, though it cannot boast a pick-proof cylinder, is so baffling as a total unit that it appears to be virtually invulnerable.

These are the hazards that the pickman sometimes faces. Unfortunately for us, he more often faces standard locks and cylinders that are quite easy for him to circumvent.

On the fringe of the pickman group, and sometimes a pickman himself, is the artful dodger, the man who prefers to use a tall story rather than a pick to get into our homes. One day he may be the meter man, next day he may be delivering a package, the day after he may be a building inspector, and the day after that he may be a polltaker or a bewildered stranger asking for directions. Whatever his guise, his objective is to get into his target area through some dodge. Once inside the door, he either takes what he can grab on the spot while the homeowner's attention is diverted or makes a swift survey (possibly including the snatching of a key or the loosening of a lock) to facilitate a return trip. It is rare indeed that he is armed or resorts to violence. If he does use violence, he loses his dodger status; the true dodger, if suspected, seldom panics into an attack. He is good at dodging out as well as in. The man who enters on a ruse and then uses violence is not a burglar. He is either a robber, or a weirdo whose primary interest is something other than loot.

Some burglars use the dodge as an occasional rather than a standard technique. These people overlap into the second major group of burglars.

The second kind of burglar is the non-pickman, the fellow who hasn't the brains or the desire or perhaps the connections to learn pickwork and obtain the necessary tools. His group includes professionals, semi-professionals, and amateurs. Most of the latter are young and may or may not turn out to be repeaters.

The professionals and near-professionals of this group do have some kind of skill. It may be a facility for filching keys and getting them duplicated, or a neat trick with a pair of pliers, or a deft thrust with a thin blade, or a sure hand with a slim crowbar, or a swift movement with a celluloid strip, or a way with a glass-cutter on a window pane. These are the manipulators. They get into their chosen target area fairly easily when given a little time and other helpful conditions, such as unkeyed windows, poor door frames, inadequate locks, and privacy in which to work.

Even the non-professionals soon become adept with the "loid." This is often the well-known celluloid strip, but it otherwise may be a credit card, or bank calendar card, or a strip· from a Venetian blind, or any one of a number of similar objects that can be slopped between door and frame at the lock area to slide back a springlatch. The loid is widely used in cases of surreptitious entry. It is only effective against tapered springlatches, or snaplatches, that are not equipped with a deadlatching feature and are activated simply by slamming the door shut. One would think that this would limit its use considerably, but it does not. Even though nearly all springlatch installations currently in use include a horizontal deadbolt that can be locked with a key from the outside, thus voiding any tampering with the springlatch, an extraordinary number of people do not bother to use this deadbolt feature when they leave their homes.

Amateurs and professionals alike will use the loid when they can and force when they must. Force does not necessarily take any kind of skill at all. A screwdriver or caseknife or some kind of jimmy is frequently used. The vast majority of burglars belong to this loid-using, force-using group. Only too often, they find their task extremely easy.

If this type of burglar is in the upper percentile of his group he will, like the skilled pickman or artful dodger or Park Avenue thief, operate as far as possible from his own home. If he is the standard semi-skilled pro or unskilled amateur he will think more of immediate gain than later getaway, and may operate across town from his own home or in the apartment across the hall.

An overwhelming majority of this common burgling type are addicts. This is not always true in suburban and rural areas; but a number of police officers in several major cities estimate that 85 percent of all burglaries are currently being committed by addicts—generally the least skilled of all burglars.

The addict will steal anything he can get away with: money, jewelry, silverware, cameras, binoculars, clothes, furs, TV sets, radios . . . any and all appliances, and whatever else he can find that looks salable. He may be armed; he may be desperate; he may resort to violence.

Somewhere on the misty borderline of this group is the prowler-burglar, sometimes an addict and sometimes not, who preys on unprotected people as well as property. Usually he grabs whatever he sees that takes his fancy—cash, if he can find it, food from the refrigerator, souvenirs from the lingerie drawer—but his basic interest lies in sating his own peculiar appetite. Hatred and violence are his middle names. He often kills, frequently with appalling sadism. This man is not a burglar in the true sense of the word.

There is another group, a third, that engages in burglarious activities but cannot be classified as belonging to the burgling fraternity because their thievery is a sort of by-product of their regular work. These are insiders, opportunists, occasional thieves; people who are, simply, dishonest, and will grab an illegal buck any way they know. They are neither professionals nor needy amateurs nor twisted invididuals looking for a kick, nor do they exist in any large numbers. But they do exist. They come in the shape of apartment house superintendents, janitors, handymen, doormen or other supervisory or maintenance personnel who have access to master or duplicate keys, and their trick is to use their privilege of access to take advantage of the tenants' absence to rifle individual apartments or whole rows of them. A man with a master key, or two men working together, can swarm through a dozen or so apartments during a lunch break.

But—the sceptic may inquire—aren't insiders bound to be suspected in a case of this sort? Yes, indeed they are. But where's the proof? The police know that a good pickman or two can do the same job just as quickly. So can the outsider who has somehow managed to gain access to duplicate keys or master keys. In many apartment house setups it is quite easy for outsiders and insiders alike to get their hands on the apartment keys and either use the originals at once or "borrow" them for copying. So, while the insider may lend himself to ready suspicion, it's not all that easy to put the finger on him . . . especially when many of the apartment doors have not been properly locked but simply snaplatched.

It may be some consolation for the wary householder to know that only a minimum of surreptitious entries are effected through the use of master keys, duplicate keys, or manipulating keys of any sort. "Skeleton" keys or "pass" keys are not nearly so widely used as some pessimists seem to think, nor are they capable of opening anything more than the simplest of locks. In fact, the burglar is seldom the clever devil that we seem to think he is.

Most burglars, excepting those who are very skilled and bold or verging on the weird or mindless, prefer to operate in an uninhabited apartment, house or store. Many of them, even the technically unskilled, have more sense than their victims when it comes to planning ahead. Any burglar with the sense that he was born with will—even if he isn't very bright or very ambitious—make preliminary surveys of his target area.

Let us first take a look at the rare bird, the sophisticated one who preys upon the rich and has all manner of techniques at his disposal.

He makes a point of reading the society columns of the big-city newspapers to find out who is taking a cruise to the Bahamas and when; who is getting married and where; who is throwing a charity ball and is very much occupied with preparations; who has died and when he will be buried, leaving a home vacant during the funeral; and who is packing up house to spend the summer, or even the weekends, in the country.

He does his homework, this near-gentleman thief. He keeps tuned to the grapevine and finds out who has bought what fabulous figurine or painting at an auction, who showers his wife with emeralds and diamonds, who keeps his money in a safe at home. Then he makes it his business to learn as much as he can of the habits of the wealthy man and his family.

He gossips with the neighbors and the neighborhood merchants, with the maid, the chauffeur and the butler (do people really have such staff these days? some do, and if they do, the smart burglar will manage to get to know the help), or he "cases the joint" in the guise of repairman or what he needs to know about the habits of the household and the kind of locks he will have to pick at a given opportunity.

If he is very bright and ambitious, and his target household contains really plummy pickings, he may contrive to get himself employed as butler/chauffeur/gardener/houseman or whatever is being hired by the rich these days. Or, if he is as much conman as burglar, he may even manage to ingratiate himself into the family social circle or perhaps go so far as to get himself engaged to aging Ugly Sister.

So much for him. His is not a common species, nor are most of us wealthy enough to warrant quite this much attention. We are observed by somewhat lesser breeds of thief, ranging from those who'll snatch at any opportunity to break in through a window to those who prowl apartment house corridors to those who emulate, in some degree, the tactics of the master-thief.

Perhaps this man takes a glance at the local weekly (say, the Bay Ridge Spectator or the Leadsville Ledger) over his morning coffee. Later he strolls out to see if the Lindstroms have indeed left for Minnesota to visit their married daughter or if the Taylors have indeed departed on their annual spree to New York City. He may then, between other small jobs, and possibly wearing something that looks vaguely like a uniform, prowl around the Lindstrom or Taylor home to make sure that no one is caretaking in the absence of the householders. If the place is uninhabited he makes a careful survey and plots his course of entry. A vulnerable back door, side door or rear window is particularly cheering to him. Now he will observe the regular comings and goings in the neighborhood, and be back later at his convenience.

If he is not one for newspaper reading he will make up for it by simply keeping his eyes open as he prowls a likely neighborhood . . . possibly even his own. He knows when his own neighbors in 4F go out to work in the mornings; he knows what the rest of them do all day. He can easily dig out similar information for other buildings in the nearby blocks.

On his reconnaisance trips around town he looks for houses that appear to be temporarily uninhabited. He notices with pleasure that the house on the corner of 18th and Elm is taking on the seedy look of a vacation-abandoned home: there are newspapers and milk bottles piled up at the front door, and mail is spilling from the box; the lawn is ragged (or the leaves are piled high, or the driveway is deep in unshoveled snow), and the windows are all closed and shaded. Maybe one dim light is burning, even during the day. If he is careful, he will come around again that night and maybe once more the following morning. If nothing has changed, it is reasonable for him to feel quite safe in making an entry at a quiet time of day or night.

However, he does not necessarily look for a house that apears to be empty for days on end. He may simply note what time the householder goes to work, what time Mother takes the children to school, and make a quick entry during their absence. If he is a little on the impetuous side he may need no more than the sight of an open and empty garage to feel free to make an attempt on the house. If someone comes to the door, well, no harm done. If no one comes, all he must do is find a fairly well concealed and flimsy entry point, work fast, and keep his eyes and ears open.

Concealment is easier than you might think, since one's neighbors seem to have been born blind or developed a fierce determination not to get involved in anything that looks at all like someone else's trouble. The burglar appreciates these people. Also, he likes a nice thick hedge around the house rather than an open expanse of lawn. He goes for a back door that has been prettied up with surrounding shrubs, and he has nothing at all against a basement window—which he often finds unlatched—swathed in shrubbery and weeds, or an attic window that is both reachable and concealed by a lovely old tree. He avoids the front door when he can, although that isn't always possible.

In some cases he tends to like one-story houses because first-floor entry is easier than second-floor entry and because he can work more quickly on one floor than two. In others, he may prefer second-story windows to those on the ground floor, because he has found that these windows are less visible to the casual, or accidental, viewer. If he has a choice between an easily accessible front window looking out over the street and a slightly less accessible side window that faces on a hedge or a bland wall or a garage, he will choose the side window every time. And, naturally, if he sees a likely looking window, he will be delighted to find a ladder lying around in the yard or in the poorly-padlocked garage.

Ranch-style houses are popular with some burglars. Many such houses have sliding doors opening onto a sun patio or porch; these doors are usually easy to open unless equipped with a superior lock. Any glass-paneled door or French window-door is a tempting invitation to the lazy, unskilled burglar. All he needs is freedom from interruption for a very few minutes, and he's home and away. Picture windows, unless they are of heavy plate or other special glass, are very attractive to him too. Quite often, glass doors and windows are attractively framed in greenery, which offers excellent cover. Most glass is easy to cut or break. Adhesive tape, which takes no skill to apply, is wonderfully portable, and it not only muffles the noise of breaking glass but holds the pieces together until the thief is ready to pick them out and reach his hand in.

Again, if the burglar is lucky enough to be able to work, even for a few minutes, without being seen or heard, he enjoys an opportunity to get at a door that opens inward. He likes the inward swing because if the door resists him and he gets impatient, he can speed up entry by kicking the door in.

If he is particularly daring or particularly desperate he may enter an inhabited house at night, or a house that he has carelessly assumed to be empty because of the absence or dimness of a light. Any nighttime burglar will aim for the dark areas every time. Light shining in or from the house, light shining on the house and garden, light spilling over possible entry points from outside sources, is something that he prefers to avoid. In the absence of such light he will make a stealthy, unseen entry. If he is aware, or begins to suspect, that there are people sleeping in the house, he will avoid the bedrooms and steal what he can from the rest of the place.

Most burglars, fortunately, are not quite so daring. Many will be deterred by a streetlamp shining outside an otherwise desirable house or by a bright light at the door. The majority of nighttime burglars prefer to work in places that they know to be uninhabited and that are not illuminated in any way. The only kind of light that they regard with some scepticism is the dim little glow that comes on night after night, going off with the dawn, in a house that shows every other sign of being temporarily deserted.

Obviously the easiest of the daytime burglaries are those committed while householders are on vacation or at work. Many burglars prefer to operate in the daytime. They are actually less visible during the day that at night because of the normal hustle and bustle of the daytime world. It is easy for them to mingle casually with the local scene and learn the habits of their prospective victims; it is easy for them to pretend that they are on legitimate errands if anyone should see them. Furthermore, most burglars know something of their local law. This varies from state to state, but in general the penalties are highest for entering an occupied private dwelling at night, less for daytime entry into unoccupied premises, and still less for entries or entry attempts that cannot be proved as actual burglarious acts. In other words, if an unauthorized individual is found loitering suspiciously in the corridors of a hotel or apartment house, he may possibly be charged with criminal trespass but he cannot be charged with the more severe crime of burglary. Only if he is found to have entered and remained in private premises through force or surreptitious act can he, as a rule, be hauled in as a burglar.

The best opportunities and the best pickings for the daytime burglar are to be found in apartment houses. There is a lot of coming and going through apartment houses (except of the very elite variety) throughout the day. The outside doors are often open, delivery men are expected, salesmen call, housewives rush out on errands, and people visit back and forth from apartment to apartment. The apartment house burglar has a ball, particularly if he is a skilled pickman or the friend of a dishonest handyman who hands out duplicate keys. Even if he is not that lucky, he often finds great scope for his loid; and if he is lucky in other ways he will quite often encounter unlocked doors, left in that condition by housewives who have gone down to the basement to do the laundry or nipped upstairs to gossip with a friend.

Prime Targets and Times

Most residential burglaries take place in apartment houses. Particularly relished by the burglar (if not by the mugger, purse-snatcher or pervert) is the apartment house without an elevator. Next in order of desirability is the multiple dwelling, which in effect is a small apartment building. Then comes the one-family house, then the two-family house. Hotel rooms and rooming houses are fairly low on the list, but nevertheless they are quite well-established on it. Cheap rooming houses, flophouses and plush hotels are better target areas for the thief than the medium-cheapies. A great many residential entries are made through the front door, in spite of the fact that the thief prefers to avoid this point of entry when breaking into a house. His favorite hunting ground, the apartment, often offers no other way in; but it does present him with so many other advantages that he can overlook that one little drawback.

The majority of reported entries are neither subtle nor sophisticated. Most are achieved through jimmying, prying, loiding or shimming. The method next in order of frequency, though quite far behind, is entry through unlocked doors, windows or transoms. Physical force, including smashing, hacking and chopping, comes next. Last on the list is the use of an unknown instrument, such as a pick, a master key, a duplicate key or a skeleton key . . . or perhaps a pair of well-bent bobby pins.

It is usually during the small hours of the morning, in the deep darkness before dawn, that the nervous householder hears creepy noises coming from doors or windows or another room. However, it is relatively rare for home burglaries to occur between midnight and 8 a.m. Late afternoon to midnight is a more popular time, although it may run a little later in particularly prosperous neighborhoods where people dine fashionably late and then hit the nightclub or midnight-party circuit. The burglar usually goes home when most other folks do. After midnight he can ordinarily expect to find houses occupied and therefore less attractive. Only the exceptionally skilled and bold, the desperate or the deranged, will deliberately work after the witching hour.

The hours from 8 a.m. to 4 p.m. are the burglar's best. More burglaries take place in daytime than after dark; daytime burglaries are increasing at an incredible rate.

The daytime burglar goes to work when everybody else does: right after breakfast, or at about 8:30. He may even carry a briefcase or some other businesslike prop. With a little luck, an observing eye and some good planning, he can time his visit to occur after the mail has been delivered and while the lady of the house (or apartment) has started on her daily errands. His prime working hours, he has found through experience, are from 10 a.m. to shortly before 3 p.m., or whatever time the kids come home from school. He can easily adjust himself to the patterns of working couples, childless families, the idle rich or the busy rich, the struggling young student couple, the career girl, the unemployed male with a working wife . . . indeed, to any type of victim in every kind of home.

Frequent contributory factors to both daytime and nighttime burglaries are improperly secured entry points, lack of an alarm system, and general unawareness on the part of the householder in regard to basic security precautions.

The majority of reported commercial burglaries take place in grocery and other food stores, factory warehouses, school buildings, diners and luncheonettes, clothing stores, bars, candy stores, small jewelry shops and drugstores. Most of these thefts occur, as might be expected, at night, when management and staff are off the premises. The greater number of these night burglaries takes place in the hours between midnight and 8 a.m. Places like supermarkets are much more frequently robbed, and by the cartload, during the day.

Basically, the means of entry into commercial establishments are the same as the means of entry into residences. Means chosen are, in this order: Jimmying or prying open a door or window; hacking, chopping, or using other somewhat extreme physical force to break through door or window; throwing an object to smash open a glass door or window; entering through an unlocked door, window or transom; using an unknown instrument to effect surreptitious entry. Because of the nature of many commercial enterprises there is some emphasis on front-door entry, or entry through glass store fronts. Entry techniques, however, are seldom anything special. Usually only banks and exclusive jewelry stores are treated to visits by super-thief. However, too often the small businessman assumes that he is not a target; too often he fails to protect himself with even the most basic of alarm systems or security gates; and too often he comes into his place in the morning to find his goods gone and his cash register empty.

The above sketch of the burglar and his preferences suggests only a general pattern of what the man and his trade may be. But, in fact, each burglar—every single one—has his own set of peculiarities, his own personality quirks, his own modus operandi by which his work can be spotted and pinned onto him.

Burgling trademarks are startlingly characteristic of the man who leaves them. They can be dead giveaways. Regrettably, they do not always lead to capture; but a look at the M.O. of several criminal types and a number of individuals may bring home to us the very urgent need to learn a great deal more about protecting ourselves. To see the thing—the mark, the eerie telltale clue—in print is a whole lot safer than seeing it in our own living room.

CHAPTER THREE

MODI OPERANDI

The modus operandi of each burglar, skilled and unskilled, has two aspects: the man's work methods, and the man's personal idiosyncrasies. His work method will fall into one of a number of fairly well-defined categories, such as picking, jimmying, removing set-screws, door-trying, drilling and so on. Once he finds himself reasonably adept and successful at a particular method he will stick with it until it fails him or he broadens his field of nefarious knowledge. (One stretch in jail can do wonders for a man's education.)

Similarly, the burglar who commits a strange, offbeat, or destructive act will tend to make it a pattern; he will do it again and again. He, too, will employ a particular method of entry for all or most jobs, but in addition he will commit a characteristic telltale act that is not directly connected with the crime of burglary. Such an act may be irritating, costly (in terms of damage), ugly or blood-chilling; whatever it is, it goes along with the man and is his trademark.

This is not to say that only offbeat burglars leave personal trademarks. Even the "normal" thief has, like everybody else, a set of personal characteristics, one or more of which may be so ingrained and so overt that it identifies him almost as accurately as his own fingerprint—although of course it does not have anything like the same value as hard evidence.

Job Categories and Practices

Not even burglars like to be lumped into categories, but the fact is that they do lend themselves to classification as one of the following:

Pickmen

First in the hierarchy though smallest in number are these skillful operators. Here we have the individuals who work on information received or on information they dig up for themselves through observation of the neighborhood, reading the papers, following the victim to acquaint themselves with his habits, and often making preliminary, "Is Mrs. Crumlish there?" phone calls, to make sure that no one is at home.

The burglar of this type is fairly quick-witted and quick of tongue. If someone answers his probing phone call he will be ready with a question or apology or other conversational gambit; he will not hang up, because he feels that this may arouse suspicions. (Potential victims among readers may, correctly, draw the conclusion that wrong numbers or nonsense calls are not always as innocent as they seem.)

Having determined that the coast is clear, our pickman goes to work with his selected tools on the lock cylinder of the door, gently stroking and maneuvering its tiny inner parts until he releases the locking mechanism. This may take perhaps fifteen minutes or perhaps five seconds. If it takes as long as fifteen minutes it is either a pretty good lock, though not by any means the best, or he is lacking in experience. He knows that hanging around a door for that long is liable to attract attention. A good pickman can usually make his entrance a whole lot more quickly than that.

Some pickmen buy their tools, some make their own. Some delight in finding ingenious ways to hide their picking tools on their persons. One pickman, currently at large, is known to use a homemade pick so small that he can—and does—carry it in a hollow tooth. In fact, this little trademark of his had become so well-known that he is probably racking his brains even now to try to come up with some new place of concealment.

Drill-and-Shim Operators

These individuals are quite rare but they do exist. Their technique consists of drilling a tiny hole immediately above the keyway of the lock cylinder and inserting, into this little hole, a very delicate piece of shim metal. The mainspring of a watch is often used for the purpose. The burglar then lifts the locking pins into position with a lock-pick and uses the tiny little piece of metal to hold them in place. Usually this burglar is not considered as skilled as the pickman, who does his work without drilling—unless he meets up with a particularly resistant lock, in which case he is not above resorting to the drill-and-shim method.

Key Holders

This group specializes in using bona fide keys, obtained in a number of ways, or going around with keys that may or may not fit whatever doors lend themselves to an attempt.

The members of this group operate primarily in hotels and apartment houses where master keys are used. What they like particularly is to gain access to an apartment house still in the course of construction. The key-burglar will use his guile to steal a mastered lock cylinder, then take it apart and make a master key with which he will have the run of the apartments when the building is completed. If he is particularly adept, and is given the opportunity, he can actually decode a lock on an established door without even taking it out. Many locksmiths cannot do this themselves, but it can be done.

These individuals also manage to get their hands on carelessly-guarded master keys, make quick impressions of them on wax, soap, clay or other appropriate material, and then cut copies for themselves. The less adept among the keyholding lot carry a wide range of keys, gathered from here and there, and visit one building after another in the hope of finding mastered locks that correspond to heir keys.

Set Screw Looseners

In this group we encounter a fairly skilled type of dodger-burglar who takes his opportunity to go to work while the door is open and the householder is intent on other things—perhaps looking for a purse to pay for a delivery, or perhaps in another room innocently assuming that the caller is an accredited individual doing an inspection of some sort. This man will quietly loosen the set screw which holds the lock cylinder in place, then go away to return later in the absence of the tenant. He will then unscrew the lock cylinder from the door and insert his finger or a screwdriver into the hole to withdraw the locking bolt. The door unlocked, he enters.

Cylinder Pullers

These burglars, who may be said to have some little skill and knowledge, make a practice of forcibly removing lock cylinders from doors with a suitable wrench or pair of pliers. An individual of this sort may become known by the particular tool he uses. Once the cylinder is removed, he follows the pattern of the set screw loosener and inserts a finger or other tool to withdraw the bolt from the lock strike.

Window Watchers

This lot has a fair amount of skill but not a great deal of daring. They make sure that no one is at home before they make their attempt, and then they choose the window at which they are least likely to be seen. Such a window may lead to the basement, or directly from the garage to the house, or may look out upon a featureless wall.

Some window watchers are at their best with a glass cutter, particularly if they are reasonably sure that they can get away with a little bit of noise. They cut away a small piece of glass in the area of the latch or bolt, preventing the glass from falling by judicious use of sticky tape or a suction cup, and then reach inside to manipulate the latch or bolt and thus "unlock" the window.

Another kind of window-watcher uses a wire. A man of this type is not particularly clever, but he does have some primitive skill. Quietly, he drills a little hole in the window frame at a convenient place, inserts a length of stiff wire to poke at the window latch, and usually manages to turn it and thus "unlock" the window. He is the drill-and-shim operator of the window watchers group.

A man with lesser skills and a minimum of equipment

may simply break the window with a stone, hammer or other tool wrapped in a wadding of soft cloth to muffle the noise. He may or may not use adhesive tape (or even sticky flypaper) to keep the pieces from dropping out and shattering noisily while he works; it depends on the working conditions. Or this man of minimum skills may look for a loosely set window whose two sections are held, not very closely together, with the common type of turnlatch. All he needs to do is slide a knifeblade between the two sections of window, flick at the keyless turnlatch with the blade, and push it out of its holding slot.

Door Triers

These unskilled operators, nearly always daytime burglars, sometimes try their luck on houses in one of those areas where "*we* never have to lock our doors; nothing ever happens here," and sometimes their attempts pay off.

More often, though, this breed of cat will work an apartment building, because he knows that here his chances of finding several unlocked front doors within a limited area are pretty good. He also knows, as pointed out above, that he is less likely to be noticed or challenged in an apartment house. He simply wanders up and down the stairs and through the hallways, trying the doorknobs to find an unlocked door. When he does, in he goes. Sometimes he locks himself in, sometimes he does not. In any event he works quickly, looks for cash and small portable items, and just as quickly leaves.

The brassier individual of this variety is not a "he" but a "she." "She" sometimes doesn't hesitate to enter an unlocked apartment even when she hears someone moving around in a back room. If spotted and challenged, she manages a look of acute surprise and embarrassment, and produces a ready story, for example, "Oh, I *beg* your pardon, isn't this the Smedley apartment? Isn't Alice here? Oh, I *am* so sorry."

Loid Users

Loid users are one step up from door triers in terms of skill and possibly one step down in gall. Rather than try knobs they ring doorbells, and have their little story ready in case anyone should answer. If no one comes to the door they try out the latch with their celluoid strip or similar article, knowing that vast numbers of homeowners carelessly slam their doors shut to activate the springlatch and fail to double-lock.

The loid user works swiftly and silently. He slides the strip between doorframe and door at the lock area, pushes gently, and quietly depresses the latch. Now the latch is no longer engaged in the strike; the door is no longer locked; and in one more second the thief is no longer on the outside.

Force Users

This group of burglars is an unskilled lot specializing—if what they do can be called a specialty—in the use of crowbars, screwdrivers, pinch bats, automobile jacks, and a variety of battering objects. They jimmy, pry, splinter, hack, smash, chop, and sometimes even kick. Both doors and windows are vulnerable to this type of thief, particularly if the noise factor need not be considered and certainly if they are not adequately secured. Of course, given enough time and freedom of action, the force user can get into practically any building even if it is well secured, but it is rare that the man has all the luck on his side. Typically, he uses a jimmy. Less typically, he may use slightly more sophisticated tools. For instance, if faced with a wood-paneled door, he may drill a little hole near the lock, enlarge the hole with a thin-bladed saw, and then reach inside to unlock the door with the turnknob.

On the other hand, so unsubtle is the typical forcer that, on encountering either a wood-paneled or glass-paneled door, he may simply put on a thick glove or wrap a scarf or towel around his fist and strike one swift, forceful blow through the panel in the area of the lock. Then in goes the hand to turn the knob.

None of his tools are unusual and none of his techniques are skilled. Yet his crude methods are employed in an incredible number of successful entries. Oddly enough, from the point of view of the public, his messy methods are preferable to the methods of the non-force users. Apart from the fact that he may attract attention, he leaves marks that are telling evidence of forcible entry. If the victim has made some evident attempt to provide his premises with adequate security devices, and if he is insured, the signs of forcible entry will carry enormous weight with his insurance company. Without them—well, lots of luck. Also, a particular mark or set of marks left on a forced entryway may be a direct tip-off to the police as to the identity—and certainly the type—of the thief. Furthermore, if the security measures are good rather than barely adequate, this man will give up his attempts to get in.

Doorchain Springers

These birds are not particularly skilled. What they do can be done, and often has been done, by a fledgling juvenile delinquent—or by the slightly knowledgeable householder who has been chained out of the house at night by an irate wife. It merely involves unchaining a chained door from the outside. The tools used are a thumbtack 'and a rubber band. No further details will be given: it is too easy to do, and a description may encourage a rash of doorchain springing among those who haven't tried it yet. It is not so easy to do if the chain is properly installed and positioned. Some are installed in such a way that the door can be opened wide enough to permit an arm to reach in and do a little tinkering around inside. Other doorchains are vulnerable less for their positioning than for the poor quality of the chain itself or the fittings. A good cutting instrument can chomp its way clear through a soft chain if it can just get a hold on it; and sudden pressure on the holding screws can yank them right out of place.

Though a few householders now use the kind of chain that can be activated from the outside as well as the inside, most people use doorchains when they are at home. The inference is that the doorchain springer, if not a prankish kid or member of the family, is likely to be an unpleasant individual. Unlike the pickman and most other burglars, he does not make an effort to avoid householders and the possibility of violence. In all likelihood he is looking for something other than money or negotiable goods.

Personal Traits

The above types are classified according to their professional techniques and tools. There are variations, many of which will be mentioned in later chapters, but they are not so widely used as the above. In addition to their job trademarks, criminals of all varieties have their personal foibles, certain telltale marks that characterize them as much as the pick or the jimmy. It is these foibles, or habits, or peculiarities, that really pinpoint them as individuals. For instance:

Artie X always drives a Buick. This year he has chosen a dark-green one; last year it was dark-blue. On all his jobs he cruises around his target neighborhood until he spots a vacation-abandoned house, then he parks a block away at night and makes his entry through a rear door (or occasionally a side if circumstances favor it) with a lock-pick.

Jimmy V is an apartment house pickman, a jovial fellow who seems to get along well with superintendents, janitors and handymen—well enough to siphon information out of them. Unlike many other apartment house thieves he likes night jobs, the kind that he can pull when the folks are out for the evening, and it is easy for jovial Jimmy to find out when an apartment with good pickings is going to be available. He is neat in his work and leaves not a damaging mark on doors or furniture. But he has a quirk about light: He never turns on the dimmest bulb, nor does he carry a flashlight. Instead, he lights match after match as he prowls through the apartment . . . and leaves the burnt-out ends scattered all over the rug.

Joe K is currently in a prison hospital. His telltale mark became so widely known that it led eventually to his capture. In his time he was fairly skilled in the easier sort of break-ins, but perhaps he lacked sufficient skill to maintain his confidence; something, apparently, made him so nervous that he developed an ulcer. Houses were usually his target, although a weekend cottage or an apartment would be well within his scope. But wherever he went and whatever he stole, he never failed to open the refrigerator and help himself to milk or ice cream or cottage cheese, in that order of preference or whichever was available.

Annette Q is a doorbell-ringing loid user who makes her living in Detroit's big, plushy apartment houses—not so plushy that she has to be announced from downstairs when she claims to be visiting a certain tenant, but plushy enough. Her manner is gracious and assured; she is an attractive, well-preserved, youngish woman who carries herself well and wears her excellent clothes superbly. In fact, her clothes are so excellent and she wears them so marvelously that, when she comes downstairs wearing a newly acquired mink or sable, she manages to look as though the coat was made for her. Certainly she "belongs" so well that no one would dream of taking a peek under that coat to count the dresses beneath, nor would anyone have the audacity to request a glance into her exquisite handbag (previously acquired by her usual methods), which she has managed to load with jewelry from a number of apartments.

Danny G, in his late twenties, dresses neatly and unobtrusively, wears earnest-looking eyeglasses, and carries a sample case. He uses a car for preliminary cruising around a neighborhood, then takes to his feet for a closer look. His victim is the suburban or semi-urban housewife who is busy in her yard, hanging out wash or digging up weeds or chatting over the back fence with her neighbors. Danny knows that people who plan to go no further than their own yards seldom lock their doors. He enters boldly, though maintaining a superficial air of polite diffidence, and helps himself to whatever he can fit into his sample case and his pockets.

Willie B doesn't have much going for him but a crowbar, an almost infallible instinct for sensing when people are not at home, and a lot of luck. He takes on apartments, houses or stores, and he works both night and day. Always, behind him, he leaves the marks of his own particular crowbar . . . and always behind him he leaves a crumpled chewing gum wrapper.

Jerry D works with Sam and Bob. If he were a little bolder he could probably do the same job alone, but he is not bold and he never works alone. Jerry has carefully acquired an honest, grizzled look, some uniforms, and several badges and identification cards. Sometimes he carries a toolbox. He is let in on the strength of his appearance and a prepared tale, and he promptly proceeds to the basement or furnace room or whatever is called for by his story. The moment he is in he is followed by Sam and Bob, who immediately seize and tie up the householder(s). Since the three men work together, they can easily handle man and wife, woman and child, or housewife and visiting friend. Then they literally strip the house.

Nameless, but always with us, is that shifting group of youngsters that pops up in so many residential neighborhoods offering to mow lawns, rake leaves or shovel snow, depending on the season. They prefer not to do the jobs and concentrate on houses that look unoccupied. If someone does answer the doorbell they offer their services at exorbitant rates that are bound to be turned down. If no one answers to hear their story, they force their way in and turn the place upside down.

Any reader can recall other tricks or dodges that have become trademarks of particular thieves or types of thieves. There's the one about the moving van that goes off with every last piece of household goods in the absence of the householder; and the one about the phony TV repairman who comes with a pick-up slip to present, if necessary, to a maid (although he is equally happy if no one is at home), and then makes off with a most desirable TV set in no need whatsoever of repair. There's the one about the Don Juan who manages to charm his way into practically every type of residential establishment with the help of some gullible female; and the one about the "maid" who goes from job to job, working a few days at each house and departing in a fake huff or on some other pretext after having given her boyfriend a chance to duplicate the house keys. The variations are endless. But most of these tricks of the trade, characteristic though they may be of groups or individuals, are still essentially work-related.

The uniform used, the type of car driven, the color of the vehicle, the charm turned on, the lie at the doorway, the size of the jimmy, the slickness of the pickwork, the respectable look—all these, though revealing of the personality of the thief, are closely related to work styles and to the specific work on hand. These details are the features on the mug shots; they are not, in themselves, alarming. It is when the criminal leaves a trademark that is not work-related that the blood begins to run a little cold. Joe K, with his ulcer and his yen for milk products, borders on the weird. Jimmy V's carelessness with matches may be suspect in some way. Even Willie B, with his scattered chewing gum wrappers, may be a little off the beam. But these people are only on the first rung of the crazy ladder.

Sal Schillizzi, the New York locksmith most likely to be called in by the wise before a burglary is committed and by the once-bitten afterwards, has seen offbeat calling cards and heard of others that send shivers running down the spine. "They do strange things, some of these people. The things they take! Little personal things, kids' toys, penny banks, the family pet, lingerie. Yes! How do you like the one who takes used underwear? Doesn't make sense, does it? But what about the man who takes the lingerie out of the drawers and scatters it around the bedroom? And those who take something, and leave something behind? There's one who leaves cigar butts. Another leaves match covers. Another guy leaves a shiny penny. And one who sits down to eat a meal at the kitchen table—leaving the crumbs and the dishes. And we had for a while there a burglar who, it seemed, would make for the cookie jar first thing. Once in a while a man will leave an empty pint bottle and a sandwich wrapper. There's another who leaves toothpicks lying around. And others who leave something . . . something really dirty." Schillizzi shakes his head. It is hard for him, a sane and kindly man as well as a dedicated and talented locksmith, to understand some of the workings of the twisted criminal mentality.

It is hard for others, too. "Yes, these are weird people," another locksmith agrees. "It's hard to know what's in their minds when they do some of these things. One thing you know, it isn't normal. Like when they apparently try on a woman's clothes. Or spill perfume around the place, or smear lipstick on the mirrors. There's odd cases that I've heard of . . . well, for instance, a fellow may use a person's toilet bowl and then not flush it. Or maybe he even deliberately dirties the floor. For what purpose? Is he mad at society? Jealous of the person's home? Is he trying to say, "— on you?" Some of the twisted minds that get into people's homes! Sometimes they write obscene messages on the walls. Sometimes they empty things out of the closets and bureaus and throw them around the house. Some of them take the cleaning stuff out of the kitchen, the liquid and the powder stuff, and pour it all over the place. Sometimes they even break up the furniture. What *are* these people?"

Back to Schillizzi: "Believe me, when an entry of this kind is made and these telltale marks are left behind—when a person realizes that there was an intruder in their home and that not only was he a burglar but he was in a sense a maniac—then he goes into a kind of shock. The realization that there was somebody in your home who would do this irrational thing, that really gets you. What would you have done, what would he have done, if you had been home or come home while he was there? Sure it's a frightening thought. People who would dirty in the middle of the floor! Or sit down at your table and eat food! A man who would do that has got to have nerves of steel . . . or something. This is not the inexperienced burglar, now. He knows the homeowner's coming back sooner or later. He doesn't care when. He's hard, he's used to it, and so what if she does come in? He'll take care of that, too. These things are happening all the time. It's not just to protect our property that we make our homes into jails. It's to protect ourselves. And don't forget that we're just talking about burglars, burglars with some kind of kink. That's not even to mention the desperate addict, the rapist, or the thrill-killer. . . ."

All of whom leave their marks, too; their dreadful telltale signatures.

39

Schillizzi also points out that it never pays to underestimate the ingenuity of thieves, eccentric or otherwise. They may not on the whole be very bright, but they have their own kind of resourcefulness and cunning. Even people who are very careful about their door locks, their windows, their fire escapes, their peepholes, and the strangers who come to their doors, occasionally overlook other factors because it simply doesn't occur to them that it is possible for a thief to make use of them. It is not uncommon for a slightly built, athletically inclined thief to make his way into a place through a very high, very narrow transom that hasn't been opened in years. Nor is it unknown for a thief to enter an apartment by means of the antiquated dumbwaiter. What can the tenant do? Secure the transoms; preferably seal them. Block the dumbwaiter doors; or better yet, get together with other tenants and the landlord and have the rope and platform removed and the shaft permanently closed. There is probably no burglar in existence who will choose transom or dumbwaiter entry as his favorite M.O., but neither is there a burglar in existence who will overlook these means if they are available and suitable to him.

Too many people, according to locksmiths and police officers alike, feel that their home is safe from burglary, particularly in the daytime, if they are there to guard it. The artful dodge may not be the most common of M.O.'s, but it is common enough for us all to take it very seriously. It may be as trivial as a pair of fake nuns collecting a couple of dollars for a nonexistent charity, or it may be something very much more serious . . . something that could happen to *you*. Remember Jerry D? There are a number of points to be made out of his story. One: Never open your door to strangers; use your peephole and your doorchain properly. Don't expect them to take the place of other security devices, but *do* use them to interview callers. Two: Check identification with the purported home office if you have not yourself requested the delivery or inspection of whatever it may be. Three: With the chain still in place, take your own good time in checking credentials. If your unexpected caller starts trying to force his way in under your very eyes you can pretty quickly slam the door shut and start to scream. Four: If you think it's safe to let in a stranger just because your husband's home or you have a friend with you, think again. You may be letting in Jerry . . . and Sam . . . and Bob.

Meanwhile, back in the department of locked doors and thieves with peculiar habits, we run into situations that at first glance suggest almost uncanny ability on the part of the thief. To illustrate the oddities that enter the lives of locksmiths and homeowners alike, Sal Schillizzi offers an account of what looked like an entirely new M.O.

A single woman in a nice old apartment house asked a locksmith to install a new lock on her door after hearing of a neighborhood burglary scare. He did so, selecting a cheap copy of the Segal-type lock (the original of which is a fine locking mechanism with vertical deadlocking bolts) and installing it meticulously. He placed it—necessarily, because of the "hand" of the door—with the bolts locking from bottom to top, checked it out to see that it was working properly, and left.

Miss A thereupon went about her normal business, which consisted of going to work every morning at 8:30 and coming home every night at 6:00. After a few days of this routine she was in a state bordering on panic. One morning early, before going to work, she put in an hysterical call to another locksmith—Schillizzi—and told him about the very mysterious goings-on at apartment 8G. Sal hurried over to get the details and make repairs. Every morning upon leaving her apartment, she said, she would lock her door from the outside with her key—she *swore* she did that every morning—and every evening upon returning home she would find the door unlocked. Nothing was ever taken from the place. In fact, so far as she could tell, nothing was even touched. But how could she be sure of that? If it were possible for someone to unlock her nice new deadbolt lock without any sort of mark, and do it again and again, how could she be sure that he wasn't doing something equally surreptitious inside? And maybe some night she would come home and find the mysterious stranger waiting for her. . . .

To Sal, it was an unusual situation. Night after night? Very strange. Nothing taken? Extremely odd. He went to work on the lock. It was not the kind that he would have recommended, but she had paid good money for it and wanted a new cylinder rather than a new lock. Someone, she thought, was apparently entering with a key or a pick; thus the obvious thing to do was to change the cylinder for a better one, which Schillizzi did. He completed the job and stepped back for an instant to admire his work. There, see? It's locked. All fixed. Now that ought to hold—!

It was 8:45. The bolts dropped down with a click—and Schillizzi's jaw dropped with them. The door was unlocked again.

After a moment of blank confusion he became aware that he had heard another sound, a much louder one accompaied by its own little click—the sound of a nearby door being slammed and double-locked.

Mystery solved. It didn't take long to discover that Miss A's neighbor, Miss B, left for work every morning about fifteen minutes after Miss A. And every morning she would slam shut her door to engage the springlatch, turn her key and her outside lock, and depart—having locked her own door and unlocked her neighbor's at the same time. The slamming of Miss B's door caused enough of a vibration to drop the bolts down on Miss A's inferior lock—even with its improved cylinder—and unlock the door. Says Schillizzi, "It's a good thing I saw it with my own eyes. Otherwise I don't know what that poor lady would have done."

What Sal himself did was to explain the mystery and change the entire lock for a better one, one of sturdier material and with a more reliable type of spring. Miss A confessed, after it was all over, that she had begun to have neurotic fears about her previous locksmith. Since he had been the one to install the lock, she thought, he must be the one who was sneakily circumventing it. Why would he do that? Well, since nothing was ever taken, maybe he was a psycho of some sort . . . maybe he just liked to be in a woman's apartment . . . maybe fondle women's clothes or something. . . .?

Miss A happened to be wrong in her surmise. But Miss A is not a particularly nervous woman, nor is she given to strange fancies. Though the chances of anyone encountering a psychopathic locksmith are so infinitesimal as to be virtually nonexistent, Miss A's suspicions regarding the possibility of an oddball roaming through her apartment were not without foundation. Oddballs, as we have seen, do that sort of thing. Those who roam but do not take may be described as Touching Toms. Stranger characters have been recorded in the annals of crime.

This lady's biggest mistake—which fortunately turned out not to be costly—was in waiting several days for the mystery to deepen. Something really could have happened while her apartment stood unlocked during her absence; someone really might have harmed her while she was alone at night protected only by a door that unlocked itself when prompted by a nearby thud. She was lucky that, during the time the mystery lasted, her neighbor did not choose to slam her door at night. The least of her mistakes was in thinking that a man with a twisted mind might have some sort of design upon her or on her very personal possessions. It would be a good thing if more women were to realize the potential dangers.

Women, because they are home more often than men, either alone or with children, are the most frequent victims of the burglar-prowler. And women, because they are women, are more vulnerable than men. To a degree they realize this. Yet it is astonishing how many women will open the door to a complete stranger and even let him into the house not only without checking his identity but also without even bothering to get properly dressed. Many an honest locksmith or repairman has been partly embarrassed and partly titillated by the sight of a scantily dressed female, a woman who cannot take the trouble to pull on a wrapper or robe before inviting them in to do whatever they've come to do.

Locksmiths' tales are full of such incidents. No doubt delivery men and parcel post carriers can add plenty to them. There are women, they have found, who tease and tantalize; there are women, police records show, who scream Rape! without the slightest provocation, except on their own part; there are women whose hysterical fancies endanger reputations and drive the police to distraction. There are even women who. . . .

But that's another story. Our story of the moment, of this book, is about the normal woman who bears a great responsibility for protecting herself and her children, and about the normal man who must provide his wife and family with the means of protecting themselves.

We have looked at some burglarious patterns and techniques, and we have taken a quick glance at some criminal types in action. Now let us take a closer look to see what we, in the supposed safety of our homes, are up against.

CHAPTER FOUR

CLOSE-UP ON ENTRY: THE CRIMINAL, THE LOCKSMITH AND OURSELVES

Man At Work

Watch this man attack our doors and windows.

Sometimes he will feel free to use force and make noise.

At other times he will employ tricks, or relatively noiseless manipulative techniques; or he will snatch at an opportunity presented to him by the unaware householder. On occasion he will rely on the most specialized of his skills and equipment.

The following are some—just a few—of the options he has.

Here, as we know, is one of his favorites, and this is what it looks like in action: Facing him is one of those tapered latch locks, the simple springlatch that snaps into "safety" position with the slamming of the door. Our pickman takes one of the more slender of his credit cards out of his pocket. Everybody and his brother has some sort of credit card these days, and carrying one is no cause for suspicion. Other forms of loid, including the celluloid strip itself, may be looked at askance. But not the credit card. He slides the card between door and frame, and to his pleasure there is no deadbolt but only the tapered latch. . . .

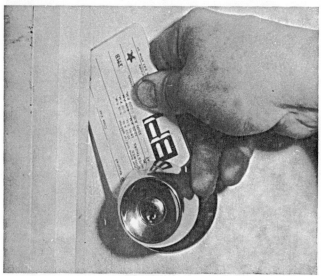

It was a breeze.

The next door is less of a pushover because it has been doublelocked. The rectangular deadbolt is firmly in place, and the lock cannot be loided or shimmed.

But is the bolt firmly in place? Our burglar notices that the door itself is not too firm, and that the frame is actually rotting slightly. He knows that the standard deadbolt is an inch long, at best, so if he can widen the space between door and frame at the area of the lock, he is in buisness. Fortunately, this door is a back door. That is probably why it has been neglected. People do tend to neglect the security of their back doors, perhaps still thinking of them in terms of "the tradesman's entrance," and therefore an entrance that doesn't matter very much. This tradesman appreciates the shortcomings of the door and the fact that he can work at it unobserved. Out comes his screwdriver. . . .

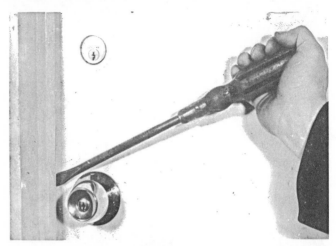

This one is even easier. We have an outward-opening door that is not a perfect fit in its frame. In fact, we can clearly see, in the crack between door and frame, the bolt securing that door. It may be possible for our man to cut through it with a hacksaw, unless it is case-hardened or of the type that spins frustratingly around when sawed at. But the old way is the best; no need for a hacksaw. Since it is such a poorly fitting door, a crowbar is much easier.

Next is another door, well-concealed from the road, that appears to be well-secured. The door is sturdy, well fitted into the frame, and locked from the outside. But the frame, though in good condition, does not appear to be constructed of very sturdy material. Indeed, one might call it flexible, which is very helpful to the thief when he happens to have brought his auto jack with him. All he does now is stretch the jack across the door from one side of the frame to the other—and then he literally stretches that frame apart. Flexible as it is, it bends slowly but does not break.

If our burglar has time, and can be bothered, he can even protect the wood from the jack by putting rubber pads on each side. In this way the jack will leave no marks. But padding or no padding, the frame soon gives enough to release the bolt from the lock strike. When this operation is completed and the home has been rifled, the thief can simply close the door again. The frame relaxes into place, the bolt re-engages in the lock strike, and if the thief has been careful there is nothing at all to show that force has been used to enter. The thief and the insurance company both win.

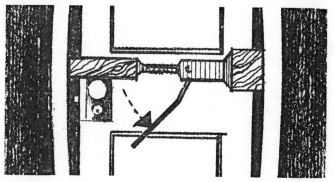

Now here's a switch: the set-screw trick.

He is making a delivery, and while he waits for the lady of the house to find her purse he carefully unscrews the set screw of her front door lock. Later in the day, or perhaps tonight, he will return to finish the job.

This time he is really in luck. He finds a door with the hinge pins on the outside. The well-heeled, the very modern and the very young probably don't even realize that such doors exist, but they do—in tenements, old apartment buildings, aging houses, and sometimes on celler entries and garages. It doesn't matter to the thief whether he opens the door from the lock side or the hinge side, so long as he can do it quickly and without being heard. In this case he is particularly fortunate because the hinge pins are removable with a very ordinary tool. . . .

The hinge side of a doorway is vulnerable even if the hinges are inside. Sometimes the screws are so short, or the door frame so old and brittle, or the wood of the door so rotten, that one determined wrench with a jimmy above or below the hinges yanks the screws of the hinge plates right out of the wood. But even supposing that both door and frame are in excellent condition, and that the hinges are inside and firmly secured with the proper screws, the door itself may be the danger spot because of its construction. If it consists of little more than a thin wooden panel, or a few layers of thin paneling, the thief might just decide to kick it in. Too noisy? Not necessarily; not if he times his kick to blend in with the innocent games of the neighborhood kids or the local construction work or the snarl of passing traffic.

Here our thief has a choice: a glass-paneled side door, and an easily accessible window looking out on the back yard. If he chooses the door he can easily cut or break the glass, then reach inside and unlock the door with the turnknob. Easy enough. But he passes up the door in favor of the window, because the window is even easier. The great majority of window "locks" in current use are not locks

at all, as the thief knows, but flimsy fastenings. The commonly used sash lock can easily be levered open from the outside, and the rubber-tipped wedge type can actually be sliced through with a knife. The wedge at this window gives . him no trouble at all.

Next is a case in which the homeowner has done an extremely foolish thing, the sort of thing that delights the heart of the take-it-easy burglar and that makes the presumably smarter folk wonder how others can be so stupid. Use an interior door lock on an outside door? Never! Well, hardly ever. Such a lock may be seen, once in a while, on a door that the owner never intends to open from the outside. There is no key to this type of lock, so the owner reasons that it can't be opened from without. But this lock, the homeowner should only know, is specifically designed to be opened without a key. Note the small hole in the center of the doorknob. Into the hole our thief sticks a medium-sized nail, a tiny screwdriver, a bobby pin or a short length of stiff wire, and turns it as if it were a key. The door unlocks at once.

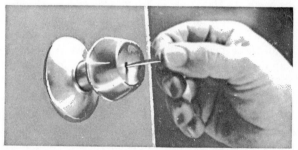

The mistake here was not made by a locksmith. This was an amateur's installation. What he did was to install a privacy lock—a lock that should only be used on interior doors to bedrooms and bathrooms and the like—instead of a security lock. There are other such privacy locks, and they must *never* be used instead of security hardware.

Facing our pickman now is the cylinder of a pretty good lock. It is a pin tumbler lock, which is the type most widely used on exterior residential doors throughout the U.S., and of its kind it is standard or maybe a little bit better. But we can say the same of our pickman: for a pickman, he's standard or maybe a little bit better. And he has a good set of tools, some of which are specially made to manipulate the pins of this type of cylinder. The pin tumbler system will be described when we are finished with our thief. In the mean-

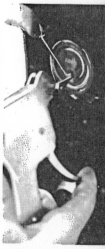

time he takes out his pick gun and a tension wrench, inserts them in the keyway, and "shoots." Presto! It is open.

The pick gun makes a series of metallic, clicking sounds, which can be eerie—and audible—on a quiet night. If our pickman is obliged to work in silence, he dispenses with the pick gun and uses a regular pick instead. One of these:

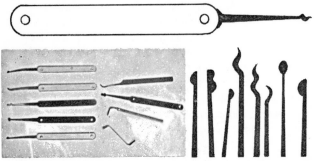

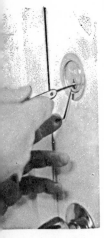

He may choose to pick each pin separately, or, if he feels he can get away with a tiny sound, he may choose to use the raking method. The latter is his present choice. He inserts the tension wrench into the keyway and follows it with the slender little pick. Now he "rakes" the wrench with the pick, in effect pushing the wrench against the pins and moving them into line. He does it almost as quickly as the homeowner does it with a key.

Most cylinders of this variety will pick, with this method, within thirty seconds. To the thief's annoyance, there are now a few excellent pin tumbler cylinders that require a very much longer time to pick. Further, there are some even more superior lock cylinders based on slightly different principles that baffle every standard tool in his collection. How-

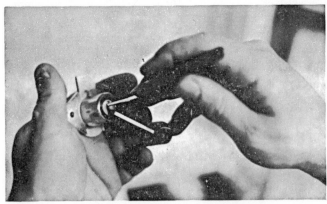

ever, to his relief, relatively few people have started to use them. Some of them don't even use the pin tumbler system.

This time it is a disk tumbler lock that our man is after. It is a medium- to low-priced cylinder that offers medium to low security—more low than medium. Our pickman rakes this lock in less than three seconds.

The lock above happens to be a brand-new one, fresh from the shop. Our skilled pickman can pick a used one of this type even faster. But who needs to pick faster than three seconds?

Next obstacle on his list is the old-fashioned bit key lock, not really much of an obstacle at all. The picks are a little different; the picking principle is much the same. Our man puts in two picks at once, applies pressure to the bolts, and lifts up the inner levers one at a time.

There is hardly anything that our man cannot open. Now he approaches a different type of lock cylinder. Because of its unusual key and unconventional keyway it offers a certain challenge. However, the expert has a special pick for this special job.

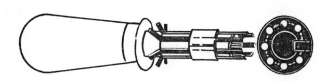

Now he finds a cellar door that looks promisingly easy. It is secured by a padlock that is pick-resistant, bullet-proof, and said to be impervious even to explosives. . . .

. . . but holds out for about a second and a half against our pickman's little fingernail-shaped shim. This little gadget of his, innocent though it looks, is capable of pushing back the locking bolt on many a widely-advertised padlock.

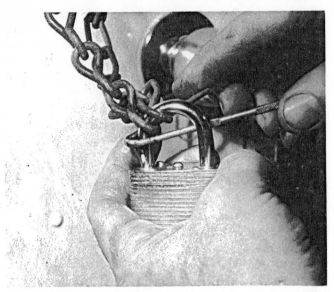

Now for the garage. There is an enormous padlock on it, so there must be something worthwhile inside. Let's see if our thief can get it out. It should be easy, really. Here is a little device, somewhat reminiscent of a nutcracker, which our thief refers to as a lock-popper—because it pops locks. See this one pop!

The above are just a few of the methods and devices used by burglars to enter our homes. It is possible to list many more, and describe them all in greater detail, but this is not intended as a manual for budding thieves. So much as we have said, any burglar already knows; to say any more might be to say too much. To know in general how a thing can be done is not the same as being able to do it, and we wouldn't want to fill in any gaps in the burglar's knowledge.

Inside the Cylinder

However, it can't hurt and it may be helpful for the homeowner to dig a little deeper into the nature of the pin tumbler cylinder that he probably has on his door, so that he can understand and believe how easily it can be picked by an expert unless it is of superior quality.

The pin tumbler lock cylinder contains a number of round pins—usually five—that are intended to be activated by the insertion of a key with a corresponding number of valley-shaped cuts. Each pin is divided into two parts, a top part and a bottom part. The top part is called the driver; it is flat at both ends. The bottom part, which retains the name of pin, is rounded or gently pointed on the lower end to fit into the little valleys, or cuts, in the key. Above each driver there is a separate little spring coil that keeps the pin forced down until something—key or pick—is inserted into the keyway. When you insert the proper key, the lower ends of the pins fit into the notches of that key. The various depths of the cuts in the key make up for the different lengths of the pins; the pins align themselves in such a manner that the separation or dividing point between each two pin segments is brought into a straight line. This cleancut separation between the top and bottom portions of the pins permits the tumbler plug, or core, to rotate within the cylinder. And when the core rotates, it carries with it the cam (a bar projecting from the back of the core or plug), which activates the boltwork of the lock.

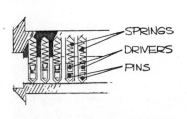

SPRINGS
DRIVERS
PINS

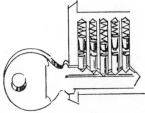

The thief who has no key must get around that deficiency either by using force, such as jimmying the door or drilling out the cylinder, or using a substitute for a key. Thus the picks, the pick gun and the tension wrench, among which the above examples are only a few of the many varieties in use. When the burglar uses (for instance) his pick and tension wrench, he is applying pressure to each pin individually, pushing each one upward and holding it there until all fall into line and the separation occurs. To make this sort of thing more difficult for the thief, manufacturers of the better cylinders usually install drivers with mushroom ends, known as mushroom drivers or spool drivers. These are shaped in such a way that, when pushed by a pick instead of a key, they tilt out of upright position and jam between the upper and lower chambers of the cylinder. This slows down the pickman . . . for at least a few seconds.

The most sophisticated "pickman" of all are, of course, our legitimate locksmiths. Picking tools are a necessity of their trade. A really first-class locksmith will supply himself with the widest range of equipment within his reach. A new type of lock cylinder is a challenge to him; a new piece of equipment is a source of gratification. His range of tools, not even including key-cutting machines of various types, far exceeds that of the criminal pickman. He has all the above, and many more. The most basic thing in his arsenal is a toolkit full of skeleton keys, which are mainly useful for the oldest and flimsiest types of locks—those which are so mass-produced and simply made that practically anything that will go into them will open them.

From this base he goes through the gamut of picks for every lock that is pickable. He has force tools, too, for use as needed; and if he is among the best of the more forward-looking locksmiths he makes sure of having the best of modern scientific equipment to diagnose problem conditions and help to cure them. With his highly sophisticated instruments he must also have almost extrasensory skills. The better his equipment, the more skilled must he be in making good use of it.

One fascinating device used by the really modern locksmith is a tiny, periscope-like device with a little light on the end. This gadget is capable of looking around small, dark corners and revealing the view to the eye of the expert. The corners which the expert is trying to probe are corners *inside the lock*. With the help of this—we will call it—little Peeper, he can literally read the innards of (for example) a safe lock.

Then there is a stethoscope—like instrument which might as well be called the Snooper, because it snoops. This is possibly the smallest bug made, although maybe the CIA has something we don't know about. It is frequently used in manipulating the combination locks on safes; some lock experts find it very useful in cylinders as well. The probe end of the Snooper, which can be inserted into the keyway, consists of a tiny mike that offers fantastic amplification to the listening ear—an ear that is listening for the sound of the pins hitting the shear line.

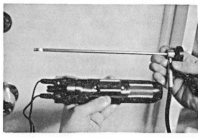

Peeper

Snooper

The Locksmith: Being One and Choosing One

Thus the go-ahead locksmith makes a point of having the best equipment and keeping up with advances in the locksmithing field. His business, as he knows, is to keep ahead of locking problems *and* the thief. It is lucky for us that locksmiths and lockmakers are unceasing in their efforts to provide us with better security products. It is lucky, too, that the man who demonstrated the above tools and techniques is not a burglar but a locksmith. He is Sal Schillizzi of New York, as honest and dedicated a man as one is likely to encounter in any profession.

So far as he is concerned, the conscientious locksmith or locksmiths' association is an unofficial arm of the local law enforcement agency. Almost as much as the police do these men have the protection of the public in their hands, and perhaps even more than the police do they have opportunities to abuse their position. The ethics, the honesty, of a locksmith are put on the line every working day. He is accepted in homes with a trust that is accorded only to members of a highly respected profession. His services are needed, at one time or another, in every type of home or business building. His specialized knowledge gives him an aura of respectability as if he were, by virtue of his position, an honest and trustworthy man.

Yet he is, after all, a man like other men. He has his troubles and temptations; he is not a saint. Sometimes he may have motives that are not readily apparent. And his opportunities to take advantage of people are mind-boggling. He not only knows, inside and out, all the locking devices that he himself installs; he knows just as much about the locks in homes he is not called upon to work on. This is something of a burden for a man. It takes a rather special kind of man to handle it. Most locksmiths are this kind of man.

But not quite all. In some few cities in some few states there are laws requiring the licensing of locksmiths, or at least there is a requirement for registering with the police. New York City locksmiths, for example, must be licensed, and the local supply houses will sell only to a locksmith with a license. Los Angeles, Miami, Portland(Oregon) and Las Vegas also have local licensing or registration laws. A few other scattered towns and counties have similar require-ments, and some major cities—notably Philadelphia—are keenly interested in the licensing procedures adopted by New York. But unlicensed locksmiths operate in all other major cities and in all our states. Most of them are just ordinary guys trying to make an honest living, and a few of them are not. The thin ranks of the latter include the full-time criminal who cannot rightly be called a locksmith at all, and the only too-human fellow who is at the mercy of the laxness, and the temptations, surrounding him.

What is unfair to the genuine, dedicated locksmith is the ease with which it is possible to obtain locksmithing equip-ment. Anyone with a little streak of larceny can easily make a quick shopping trip or fill in a mail order blank and order a complete set of picking tools for the price of one small burglary. These things are readily available. Look at the tiny ads in some of those magazines that come to you unasked or even by subscription. Write for a catalog. You could get rich.

Getting an education as a locksmith can be easy, too. You can get it through apprenticeship (hard work, but appren-tices are needed); you can get it by being a member of a locksmithing family (which is not something you can ar-range for yourself); you can get it in a locksmithing school (of which there are few, but the entrance requirements are usually none too exacting); or you can get it by mail and you can get in in jail. Depending on your viewpoint regarding what's easy and what isn't, getting it in jail or from a criminal associate is probably the easiest, and anyway the most common, way for the dishonest individual to learn certain skills that rightfully belong in the province of the genuine locksmith.

Says Schillizzi: "You should only know the problems that they're having in many states with ex-convicts passing themselves off as locksmiths because of no licensing laws! You know, we New Yorkers are pretty lucky, having licensing of locksmiths. This means that a man can't have a record of any sort and be allowed to practice locksmithing. This is good for the public and for the locksmiths too. I think that we, in this state and in this city, should encourage people in other states and other cities to write their congressmen, their senators and their local representatives to encourage licensing of locksmiths. Maybe there should even be federal legislation. But every part of this country should have it. You don't want a burglar or a potential sex offender or someone who has a shady background to come into your house. You don't want him in your home at all, and you don't want him to be the one who knows all about your locks. It would be good insurance for the public if we had licensing in general. It could be done; it should be pushed for."

Licensing is quite common for other professions throughout the States, Schillizzi notes. "Most licensing bureaus seem to turn a blind eye to the need for licensing locksmiths. And yet they turn right around and license plumbers and electricians and other people whose jobs are even less critical in terms of your security. Of course you want to know that these people are qualified. It's important, when there's a question of life and safety involved. With an electrician's work there is possible danger of fire or something, so it is vital for him to be a trained and licensed man. The same thing is true of plumbing, among other licensed trades. But in locksmithing there is life involved, too. In getting locks on your house you're concerned with safeguarding not only your own property but yourself and your family. You're concerned with keeping out the criminal, the man who may be not only a thief but a killer. There's no getting away from it. There *are* questions of danger, of life and death, involved in many aspects of locksmithing. You have a right to be sure that you are dealing with a qualified, trustworthy man. So I strongly believe that locksmiths should be licensed."

Yet it seems difficult to convince people, lawmakers and

licensing bodies among them, of the need for licensing the members of this important profession.

Let it not be thought that the man picked up with a sackful of loot and a pocketful of picks is a locksmith. He is not; he is a burglar. There are people who decode locks and cut keys for their own use or for use by fellow criminals. Again, these people are not locksmiths, nor do they set up shop to cater to the general public. They serve a select group of clients who are not looking for security hardware for their own doors, but for a quick way in through someone else's. Our best defense against these people is not a licensing law but a better lock.

Licensing, however, will help immeasurably to ensure that the locksmiths we deal with are trained, capable and reputable men. We do not, now, have that assurance.

So where does this leave us when we're choosing locks for our doors and a man to install them? Not in a hopeless position by any means. Locksmiths in general are very proud of their profession and its reputation, for theirs is one of the oldest and most honored of all professions. They are the first to take action if they have reason to believe that a colleague is engaged in any illegal activity or is undermining their profession by doing shoddy work.

Your neighborhood locksmith may have his faults, but the chances are that he is as honest as you. You can assess him yourself by going to his shop and taking a good close look at him and the kind of place he runs. In some few cities, as noted, you will be able to find a licensed locksmith. With him you can feel secure . . . as secure as with your licensed electrician. In others you might be able to get a good recommendation from the police department. In most, you will have to rely on your own good sense. A trusted friend or employer may be able to give you a lead. Otherwise you will have to check in the classified pages of your local telephone directory, locate the locksmiths in your general area, and then go to the most likely-seeming one and look over his premises.

As Sal Schillizzi puts it: "Go down to his place and see if he runs a legitimate looking shop. See what he's got by way of equipment and supplies. See what kind of man he seems to be. If he exclusively does locksmithing, you're lucky. But many locksmiths, in small towns particularly, have to have other lines as well, and here you really have to use your senses. Just see what locksmithing stuff he has, what kind of locks he offers and what kind of keys he can cut. Judge him by that, and by his manner. Don't be put off if he also sells hardware, or luggage, or something of that sort. Look around and see if he has a fair range of good-quality security hardware and knows something about it. That's the best you can do. That's the way we shop for just about everything, isn't it?"

Right. But, as he further points out, you do have one other way of assessing him—by his membership in a lock-smithing organization. Licensed or not, the qualified lock-smith who cares about his work will generally be a member of a professional association and will proudly display his membership credentials in a prominent place.

When selecting your locksmith, by all means give prefer-ence to the one who belongs to a local or national locksmith-ing organization. He is the one who is eager for new ideas, who respects his work, who keeps up to date, who is con-stantly in touch with changing techniques and new devices, and who is looking for ways to be of better service to his customers. Membership in A.L.O.A., for instance, is in itself a mark of quality. A.L.O.A. stand for Associated Lock-smiths of America (Inc.). The membership qualifications of this association are such that, when you select a member as your locksmith, you know you are getting a man with solid character references as well as thorough training and experi-ence. Through the facilities of A.L.O.A. he has access to the pooled knowledge of the locksmithing world. By attending conventions, symposiums, seminars and the like he is con-stantly keeping abreast of developments in his field. If he needs instruction in regard to a new lock or cylinder or a new idea in servicing, he can get it through this body; and if he has new ideas of his own to try out, he can try them on the experts. Many local associations offer similar opportuni-ties. The chances are good that you are making a wise choice when you select one of their members.

This still leaves us with the question of those vulnerable entryways and pickable locks and illicitly acquired keys. Locksmiths will advise you and make recommendations, but they cannot force you to take anything that you think is too expensive or too clumsy-looking or whatever. If you insist on a cheap version or copy of a lock, they will be obliged to give it to you. Understandably, you do not want to go for the ultimate in high-priced locks—but neither do you want to sell your security for a few dollars. The ease of lock-manipulation—if only you know how—is brought home in a few comments made by "Red" Rudensky, a very famous ex-con. He reformed long ago and became a highly public-spirited individual; but the new man remembers the old man

only too well. He was, among other things, an expert lockman who dealt exclusively with the criminal element during
his career as illicit keymaker. His "job," for a while, consisted in making grand masterkeys for certain expensive
hotels or elegant apartment buildings that had been chosen
as targets by (primarily) jewel thieves. It was such an easy
task, Red says, that he used to wonder why the thieves
themselves "didn't bother to learn the simple mechanics of a
pin-tumbler cylinder lock to enable them to make their own
'screws' (or duplicate keys)."

"The simple mechanics"! That is the operative phrase.
The mechanics are simple, and too many people have been
learning them not only for the purpose of making duplicate
keys but for outright picking. If they attain any degree of
proficiency they can, as we have seen, manipulate the standard pin-tumbler in minutes or even seconds.

But if you are now in a state of despair at the thought
that the standard cylinder, so widely in use and probably on
your front door right now, can so swiftly be circumvented,
bear these thoughts in mind: (a) the average burglar is not
a skilled pickman; (b) you can do much better for yourself
than the standard pin-tumbler cylinder; (c) two or three
locks are better than one lock, and if you have one that is
strongly pick-resistant and another that is jimmy-proof,
you're in pretty good shape; (d) a total plan of security,
including your perimeter defenses, your door and window
hardware, and perhaps an alarm as well, is better than the
finest single lock.

Let's take one last look at that ordinary pin-tumbler
cylinder we have picked apart in a number of ways. Is it
really so simple for the pickman to beat? Yes, it is. *But:*
There are lock cylinders with ten pins, rather than five.
There are cylinders with three *sets* of pin tumblers. There
are cylinders with pins arranged in a circle instead of in a
row. There are cylinders whose "pins" are magnets that
cannot possibly be lined up with a pick. Cylinders of this
sort, and some lock units still to be mentioned, are completely beyond the scope of even the thief with some skills.
There are means of eventually circumventing some of these
superior locks and cylinders, but they are so complex and
take so much time to defeat that only the rarest of criminals
would dare to work on them. In desperation he might drill
them out or blow them up—but that sort of thing does tend
to attract the attention of the neighbors. True, they don't
care to get involved, but they are often nosy; and if there's
one thing apart from a good solid lock or a loud noise that a

burglar cannot stand, it's a nosy neighbor.

CHAPTER FIVE

PRIMARY DEFENSES

Aspects of security for the home range from the nature of the neighborhood to the timely use of a lightbulb. If you are happily installed in your present home and have no intention of moving, then you have to do the best you can with whatever security arrangements are within your reach. But if you are currently looking for a new place to live, either apartment or house, you might as well incorporate your security needs into your overall requirements. In many ways, it is easier to start from scratch. In fact, if we could all build just exactly what we want exactly *where* we want it, we would be in great shape. But we don't all have that opportunity. Most of us have to hunt for existing accommodation that comes closest to meeting our needs. And many of us, perhaps by circumstances not too well-off or just beginning careers, must look for our homes in the lower-rent areas that do not meet our ideal security standards. But at least we can try to satisfy most of them.

Apartment Hunting: Best Bets

Most of what can be said about the security factors involved in choosing an apartment applies equally to single men, single women, and married couples. But a young girl looking for a place of her own, or two or three young girls looking for a place to share, should be particularly conscious of these factors. The young career girl, possibly new in town or at least new to the experience of finding and having her own apartment, is the most vulnerable of people because she is a target in herself. She needs to take extra care.

Reconnaissance

Two heads are indeed better than one when it comes to home-hunting. A girl apartment-hunter should always have a friend with her when looking over anything that looks like a possible prospect. The friend should be a man. The male apartment-hunter would do well to have a friend with him, too, and as you no doubt have guessed, that friend should be a girl. This is not just because it's nice to hunt in mixed pairs; it is because the masculine and feminine point of view together add up to one balanced point of view. One hunter might observe something that the other misses; the other might think of something that would never occur to the one. Besides, the girl should have male company when she first looks around the neighborhood at night.

That's right, at night. In the cheerful light of day the neighborhood, and the building itself, may put on its best face and be on its best behavior. It may be just as nice at night, which would be a point in its favor. On the other hand, either the building or the neighborhood or both may be uncomfortable dark and deserted. Street lights and other outside lighting may be dismally inadequate. The entrance to the building may be unlit, unprotected, and swathed in heavy shadow. Drunks or idlers may use the outer steps as a resting place. Or dark alleyways may offer their shadowy protection to prowlers. The hallway itself may be dimly lit, and it may have open archways or doors leading to even more dimly lit areas where the mailboxes are located. The stairway to the basement laundry room may be in total darkness, and even the upper stairways and the landings may be lit by nothing more than a dim sort of haze.

Then again the neighborhood, and even the building itself, may light up like a neon sign at night. Perhaps the sleepy looking little restaurant next door blossoms into a discotheque that keeps jumping and blaring into the small hours of the morning, and busy multicolored lights flash into the upstairs windows. That may be just fine for those who thrive on noisy nightlife, but it wouldn't do them any harm to give thought to what sort of element is attracted by the neighborhood activities . . . or to the possibility that outside noise might serve to cover up close-up sounds, such as a furtive scratching at the door or a footfall on the fire escape.

Day or night, or both, you should take a good look at the workings of the downstairs doors. Ask questions. Are the back and basement doors kept locked at night, unfailingly? And how well secured is the main front door? How it is locked and how it is guarded may not be the most vital factors in your decision to move in or not, but be sure you know the system before making up your mind. Adequate security at an apartment house entrance is a difficult problem unless the rent is high enough to pay for full-time surveillance, an effective intercom system, and perhaps closed-circuit TV. But at least try to find a building that fulfills the following requirements:

1. A good, bright outside light burning from dusk to dawn, fully lighting the doorway area and the door itself.

2. A well-lit, lobby, with all corners and alcoves adequately illuminated.

3. A front door that is kept locked at all times and can only be opened from the outside with a key, by remote from the apartments with an electric door opener, or from the inside by a doorman on duty.

4. A night man who can keep an eye on that door and be on call in case of emergency.

5. A buzzer-intercom system that really works and really is used. The building staff and tenants will tell you how effective it is—especially the tenants. There's not much use to a system that is more abused than used. If the door is regularly opened to callers by means of a returning buzz without tenants bothering to check identity over the intercom, there's little point to keeping the door latched.

If you are reasonably satisfied so far, both with the entrances and the interior lighting, have a look at the elevator. This, too, should be well-lit. If it is a self-service elevator it must have a mirror that reveals the occupants to whoever is waiting to get in. It must also be equipped with an alarm, preferably one that sets up an ear-splitting clang when activated. (Some are silent at the point of origin, releasing their signal in some distant basement room.) The noise is a deterrent in itself to anyone trying to pull a fast one in the elevator, and a loud noise that everybody can hear throughout the apartment house has a good chance of drawing help—even if it is only the irate crackpot in 2B—quickly. Another feature that is good to find in a self-service elevator is a lock, one that can be activated by the superintendent, to prevent the elevator from being called or sent down to the basement after a certain hour. This is only effective where there are no stairs to the basement or where there is a securely locked door between the basement and the main floor. The purpose of the elevator lock is to fox the thief who somehow manages to get into the basement and then seeks to work his way upstairs.

The superintendent of the apartment house deserves your close scrutiny, too. Talk to him yourself so that you can make your own character judgment and discover a few pertinent facts. Your own impressions of him are important, though certainly not infallible, and you can check your judgment against that of other people—starting with your companion on the hunt. Find out whether he works in the building part-time or full-time; whether he lives on the premises or is away at night; and how long he has held his present job. If he is away at night and no one subs for him, have second thoughts about moving in. If he has worked for several years at the same address, he is likely to be fairly dependable. If the turnover of superintendents in the building has been rather high, mark that fact on the debit side.

Make a few casual inquiries in and around the place. Sometimes the neighborhood merchants or employees of adjacent apartment houses are helpful, and sometimes they are not. If they cannot give you any sidelights on the character and reputation of your possible super-to-be, then waylay a couple of tenants. They will almost certainly be glad to talk about him. Ask the tenants about other help, too; about the doorman, elevator operator, handyman, night watchman and so on. These are all people you would like to be able to trust. The superintendent, particularly, is usually in a position to enter your apartment pretty much at will (although you can take steps to limit his freedom of access). If this man seems to be generally regarded with mistrust, then you might do well to keep on with your search. Similarly, if he is thought to be honest but careless, or trustworthy but incompetent, or pleasant but often inebriated, or clever but lazy, you might be quite right in feeling less than totally safe with him around. On the other hand, if he seems to be the only major fly in the general ointment, you may be justified in taking the apartment and being extra careful about your own security arrangements.

To get hold of an apartment in a building occupied by the owner himself may be a lucky break. Some owners are do-nothing Scrooges who either don't know how to run a building or don't mind seeing it fall apart so they can graduate to slum landlordship, but most owners who live on the premises tend to have some degree of house pride. They don't want the building broken into, any more than you do, and they want to keep it nice for themselves if for nobody else.

Far more than the absentee owner does the on-the-premises owner (usually) care about his house. Usually he has a certain regard for sanitary conditions, for good lighting, for good security and for good service. Better yet, he is on the spot and available for discussion with tenants; and he is, unlike a superintendent, in a position to take immediate action on requests . . . if he feels like it.

Moving In

When you have decided that you can, or will have to, put up with the disadvantages offered by a certain apartment, you will need to do a number of things. Possibly you will have to pay an agent's fee or offer a little getting-to-know-you gift to the super, just to make sure that he doesn't turn around and give the apartment to someone else while your pen is hovering over the dotted line. Then you sign the lease, pay a month's rent in advance, pay a month's security, and receive the keys.

At this point you get frantically busy cleaning up the place and cleaning out your old home. At the same time you get estimates from several movers, make your choice, and start doing as much as you can of your own packing because it's cheaper and safer that way. Number each package, crate, box or barrel that goes out of the house, and keep a corresponding list of these containers along with a description of the contents of each. Incorporate this list into your furniture inventory. You'll find that knowing what's in each box makes unpacking very much easier—and you'll also find that the numbers will help you make a fast inventory of every single piece before the movers leave your new place.

Now here you are, cleaning up again. You're about three months or maybe four months poorer than you were a couple of weeks ago, and all you have to show for your outlay is some cluttered living space and two or three keys to go with it. One key is probably to the outside door, which is always open anyway, the second is to your own front door, and the third (if any) is to your back door. The fact that the window leading onto the fire escape has no lock is going to be your problem, one that you are going to want to work on without delay. But the doors are your immediate problem.

Commonly, your front door will be provided with the single mortise-type unit combining a springlatch and a horizontal deadbolt lock. The springlatch automatically snaps into postion when you close the door, and the deadbolt is activated by key from the outside and—usually—thumbturn from the inside. If there is a back door it is likely to be similarly, or perhaps even more simply, equipped. The cylinders may or may not be perfectly adequate in themselves. However good they are, they have at least one drawback: they have been used by somebody else. Furthermore, it is quite likely that the cylinder on your front door at least is on a masterkeyed system, with the master key held by the superintendent.

Check your lease again and see exactly what it says. It almost certainly does *not* require you specifically to maintain a masterkeyed cylinder in your door or relinquish duplicates of your keys to the owner or superintendent so that he may enter whenever he pleases. The owner and superintendent may have the "right of access," yes, but if that's all it says in the lease on that particular subject, then you are not required to do any more than let them or other authorized parties in when you are requested to do so. It does not mean that your lock has to be masterkeyed or that you necessarily have to give out key copies.

If the lease clearly demands that your permit a copy of your key or keys to be held by the superintendent, then your choices are: one, to have that clause in the lease changed; two, not take the apartment; three, turn over the required key or keys under your own conditions, safeguarded in the manner described below. But whatever the lease requires, it is extremely unlikely that it legally obliges you to put yourself at the mercy of a masterkeyed system or at the mercy of anyone who might already be in possession of a key to your new apartment. Why should you? The previous occupant of your apartment may have kept his key, and he may not be totally trustworthy; for all you know, he may be planning to use it again. Or he may have left a copy with a friend, who may turn out to be less than totally honest. Or perhaps a thieving ex-employee of the building may have kept a copy of your key—or even of the master key.

In any event, you owe it to yourself to change the cylinder of the existing lock. Not the whole lock; just the cylinder. And get a good one. If the rest of the building is still masterkeyed and now you are not, so much the better for you. You will have the proper degree of control over who comes and goes, and you will still be able to provide sufficient freedom of access to the landlord and his representatives.

Now add another lock to your door, one of your own choosing. Get a good, jimmy-proof, rim-type deadlock with interlocking vertical deadbolts, and have it equipped with a pick-resistant cylinder. If there is another means of access to your apartment, have your door lock equipped with dual cylinders, both requiring a key to operate. The outer cylinder should be pick-resistant; the inner must be standard. This ensures that anyone entering your apartment through, for instance, a window, will be unable to leave by the front door because he requires a key to do so. A window-enterer is not a man with picking skills. The point is not so much to keep him in but to prevent him from exiting via the front door carrying his bundles with him. Even though the window through which he entered is still available, he prefers not to use it because it isn't easy to look as though you belong on a fire escape (and certainly not on a drainpipe!) if you're carrying a TV set or an armload of clothes. Walking through the halls with them is a whole lot easier. Thus, if you have locked him in, he will either have to smash his way out at great risk of attracting attention, or he will have to leave most of his loot behind him.

Naturally you would prefer that he does not get in at all, therefore you will treat your back door with the same respect as your front door. You must install a good lock on your back door, as well as a chainbolt and peephole interviewer on both doors. Seal up any transom or dumbwaiter shaft if there is the remotest chance of it being vulnerable. If you have a window or windows that can be entered from outside by any means imaginable, supply it or them with a key-operated lock. Easily accessible windows, such as those leading onto fire escapes, should preferably be secured with an accordion type gate that is easy for you to open from the inside in case of emergency but impossible for anyone but a fireman to open from the outside. But be sure, before installing bars or gates of any sort, that they meet with local regulations. Some types are dangerous; you *must* be able to get out in a hurry, and you don't want a permanent fixture or even a padlock.

To do all this you need a qualified locksmith of your own choosing, selected in the manner described earlier. Be sure that he can not only sell and install the locks you want but that he is equipped to cut extra keys for them should you need copies. (The manufacturers of some superior locks or cylinders are highly selective in their choice of locksmiths to be permitted to cut their keys.) The man of your choice should not be the locksmith preferred by the owner or superintendent of your building; he should be the locksmith preferred by you.

The superintendent or owner of your building may be slightly affronted by your decision to install a lock or locks that are not fitted to the master key. But your decision is based on your security, not on his convenience. Under the masterkeying system, all the locks in one particular building are made to accomodate two different keys. One is the master key, which opens all those locks, and the other is the tenant's change key, which activates only his own lock. This system has certain advantages and many drawbacks.

Masterkeying

The popular misconception is that a master key is a "pass" key. It is not. It is neither a pass key nor a skelleton key. Pass keys or skeleton keys are actually crude pick keys that can be made to open practically any extremely cheap or low-grade lock simply by being jiggled around in the keyway until they happen to catch the simple, single lever inside. Masterkeying, on the other hand, is generally confined to high-grade hardware utilizing pin tumbler mechanisms. A lock that is masterkeyed is designed for the purpose of permitting authorized individuals to use that lock and all others that have been similarly masterkeyed. Such a system may be set up by the key manufacturer or by a qualified locksmith. Any particular master key is issued to one building alone; corresponding masterkeyed locks and change keys are issued to that building alone. When the owners of the building require additional master keys they must put their request in writing and furnish proof that they are the genuine owners of the lock.

The pin tumbler cylinder of such a lock is in no sense intrinsically inferior to an unmastered lock. The tenant in 4F cannot use his key to sneak into 1A. The keys are not the same; the bitting is not the same; and the quality is usually quite good. The masterkeyed cylinder differs from other cylinders only in that it has an additional set of pins. This extra set of pins—the master pins—provides an additional set of "breaking points" to meet at the shear line. When you insert the correct key into a regular cylinder, the bottom pins line up at the shear line. When you insert your key into a mastered cylinder, the middle, or master, pins also line up at the shear line. Obviously, your key is still "your key," even though the lock is mastered. Obviously, too, only the correct key can open all the apartments in any single building.

Now all this sounds quite reassuring, and when the superintendent very reasonably explains that he and his men must have such a system in order to enter any tenant's apartment in case of fire or plumbing emergency, one is inclined to see his point of view quite readily.

But what does our consultant locksmith say about it?

"Take a big apartment building. Take the buildings in developments. You'll hear the superintendents say, 'My men *have* to have access to a master key in case of emergency. What if the tenant isn't home when something happens? What if he is home, and for some reason can't open the door?'

"Well, now, you don't need a master key for that. And a master key can be used in a way that's something else again. One of the staff can enter an apartment that he had no right to enter in the first place. Let's say he gets the key perfectly legitimately to enter one apartment. Then, if he is so inclined, he can use it to enter another and another. I'm not saying he will—but he can. And even if he doesn't, he may be suspected of having done exactly that. Whereas if his superior had just given him the key to the one apartment he was supposed to enter, and had him sign for it, then he would know that his man had not been in some other apartment. If there were a robbery he would be able to say, 'I did not give my man the key to that apartment, so my man was not in there.' But he can't honestly make that statement if he had simply handed out the master key. So, as you can see, there are disadvantages in masterkeying not only for the tenants but for the building staff.

"Another thing about masterkeying systems: A person can come into the building on a sublease, or temporarily on the staff, or perhaps as one of the domestic helpers; take one of the locks apart, and decode the master key. Now, with that master key, and living or working in the building, this person can have play of the entire place. The police quite often catch burglars with master keys on them, obtained in just this way or copied from the one that was supposed to be locked up. This master key system should really be reconsidered; it should be a thing of the past."

On the plus side is the genuine convenience factor— convenience for the honest, that is—that may, under some circumstances, be overriding. Masterkeying at least does away with the need for having an individual duplicate key for each apartment. It may work very well in, let us say, a fairly small building under the supervision of a superintendent whose integrity is beyond question, who keeps the master key under conditions of absolute security, and always accompanies, in person, any service individual or handyman requiring access to a particular apartment in the absence of the owner.

Even under these circumstances there is no guarantee— there is never any absolute guarantee—that a thief may not break in from the outside and then, from the inside, decode the apartment lock. But the superintendent with foresight and the cooperation of the building's owner will be prepared for such a contingency by being in a position to change the basic component of all the locks in a matter of a little more than minutes. He will have installed *removable interchangeable cylinder core* locks under his master key system. With these, if he suspects that someone may have gained illegal access to a master key, he can change every one of the cylinder cores by inserting his control key, removing the core, and inserting a different core. In effect he is changing the whole locking system—all the cores and all the keys—and making it immune to anyone who has succeeded in decoding a now-discarded cylinder. In the same manner, he can replace any single cylinder core for which a key might have been lost and possibly picked up by an unauthorized person. This makes for a great deal of convenience, although the superintendent must be doubly certain to keep his control key under strict security. When honesty and common caution are both employed, there is much to recommend this system.

But, regrettably, there are usually too many loopholes under any masterkeying system. A great number of buildings, most security systems, and many individuals just do not fulfill the basic resuirements for making masterkeying a success. The master key is only too often kept under conditions of dubious security, so that it is available to quick-fingered outsiders and insiders alike. Here are some cynical words of wisdom from another widely experienced locksmith:

"If your building is on the masterkeying system, you have no way of knowing if other people are going into your place whenever they like. There's plenty of inside burglary going on. Somebody on the apartment house staff—maybe the super, maybe some other employee—can be keeping track of your comings and goings, noting if you work the whole day or part of it, or if you go out, say, every Friday and Saturday night. He can also make note of what you have in your apartment, and what your neighbors have in their apartments. When he's sure there's no one home he can have a good look around your place, see if you have nice silver, or good clothes, or furs, or expensive furniture, or fine appliances, or elegant rugs, maybe a money chest or even loose cash. Once he finds what looks like a good haul, he can use his knowledge of your schedule and the habits of the nearby tenants and set up a burglary for a suitable time. He'll either do it himself or get someone else to do it, in which case he splits with him.

"Now the man goes in with the key. He takes what he wants and moves it out through the front door, knowing as he does when the coast is clear. Then what he does is either force the door, if he can get away with it, or break a fire escape window, so that it looks like an outside job. And away he goes. You'd be surprised how many burglaries that look like outside jobs are committed in this way. Ever wonder how thieves get out of apartments apparently unseen, lugging heavy stuff? That's one way."

And *only* one way, let it be stressed. There are plenty of bold outsiders, too, with a vast repertoire of pretexts for removing anything from a fur wrap to a grand piano.

The more thoughtful building superintendents, of which there are many, agree that masterkeying can be a pain in the proverbial place. "Who needs it?" they say. "It's not as if our men have to be running in and out of the apartments all day long. One key *at a time*, that's all that's needed." Even worse than masterkeying, as one superintendent pointed out himself, is what is called "maison" keying. This system is used in many office buildings and apartment houses; and it should not be. What happens here is that each tenant is given a key that operates not only the individual apartment or office lock but the main front door as well. This means that the coding within the lock is arranged in such a way that each lock is weakened, in a security sense, to the point that it is only too easy to circumvent.

What, then, is one supposed to do? Back to Schillizzi:

"Try for a place where the superintendent is bonded. Then you know the man's background was checked. Change the cylinder and add a second lock when you can possibly get away with it. In most places and under most leases, you can. Now if the superintendent or the management absolutely insists on a key, then you give him one. Under law in most places, they're supposed to have a key for use when absolutely necessary. That goes for your second key, too, if that's what it says in your lease. A trustworthy man will keep all key copies *locked up* in a safe, or at least in some sort of strong cabinet in a locked room. But you can give yourself more protection than that. Give him your key or keys in a sealed envelope.

"You'll want to do this particularly if your superintendent isn't bonded. You've got to remember that some supers aren't quite the sort of people who should have keys. If you feel uncertain of yours, and if he is supposed to have a key, give it to him in a sealed envelope with definite instructions not to use it unless it's vitally important. First put the key in a folded piece of cardboard, then tape the edges of the cardboard, and put this little package inside a small, strong envelope. Seal the envelope in the normal way, sign your name across the flap, and then put a piece of scotch tape over that. Removing scotch tape over a signature sort of destroys it, you'll find. Now you're going to have to check up on your sealed envelope every once in a while, but it's worth it. You'll know if the key's been used or not. And it's always kind of interesting and useful to know if anyone is going into your place without asking your permission beforehand."

A superintendent, commenting on this, found the suggestion less than ideal but conceded that it does have its points. The main advantage, in his opinion, would be the ease of proving that his men were not constantly roving in and out of apartments in the tenants' absence nor using the duplicate to commit burglaries. It would also tend to remind him, he said, to notify the tenants ahead of time, whenever possible, that he or one of his men would need to enter a particular apartment on a particular day. "Gives 'em a chance to lock up their diamonds," he said, a little sourly.

Laws in certain parts of this land require landlords of new buildings to provide security features. These, as a rule, are peepholes (door interviewers) and perhaps chainbolts; adequate exterior and interior lighting; effective locks on individual apartment doors; general (main) entrance doors equipped with self-locking mechanisms; an intercom system that permits tenants to identify any caller and then release the lock mechanism to let him in; and a mirror in any self-service elevator, permitting a view of the inside of the elevator from without. New York is quite well off in this respect. In that city, having a second lock on one's apartment door is a legal right. Buildings under construction or to be constructed must incorporate approved security features. For some buildings not covered by laws relating to new construction, landlords must provide the self-locking door and the intercom system for the main entrance if requested to do so by a majority of the tenants, who are then committing themselves to a slight rent increase.

It can pay you, therefore, to inquire closely into your city and state laws regarding the security requirements of apartment buildings. It is quite possible that your landlord is legally obliged to pay for certain features that you feel are essential to your security. It may also profit you to join, or form, a tenants' association to push for improvements, either in the shape of a full-time doorman, a more security-conscious superintendent, or a better overall security system. In fact, through meetings and discussions, tenants themselves can be made more aware of the need for care in using the buzzer-release system, and perhaps they can even be persuaded of the value of a small rent increase to pay for quite a lot more security. Even where self-locking mechanisms, intercoms, peepholes, doorchains and elevator mirrors are not required, they *are* needed. Press for them by all means, pay for them if you must, and use them when you get them. Above all, lobby for the right to put your own locks on your own apartment door.

The question of individual locks is at its most difficult when it comes to large housing projects. Many of these are fairly suitably equipped with some, even most, of the security requirements, but their tenants are rarely permitted to put their own locks on their doors. Management insists that it is essential for project personnel to be able to enter apartments with master keys. Any other system, they say, would be clumsy and inconvenient. That may be so, but there is little to indicate that they have investigated any other system or tried to find a solution palatable to themselves and their tenants. In the meantime, project tenants in many cities are being robbed left and right. Usually these are the people who can least afford any sort of loss.

Here and there you will encounter a city commission that is concerned with the problem of security for residents in projects and developments, but as yet no one seems to have been able to get over the masterkeying hurdle. No one, that is, except for an occasional spirited tenant. In one New York project the tenants got together and persuaded management to permit the use of second, unmastered locks on condition that each signed a lease absolving project authorities from all blame in case anything were to go wrong as a result. When building employees want to get into any apartment, they make arrangements beforehand. In another eastern city a fledgling lawyer told a tenants' meeting that he, personally, was going to put a second lock on his door no matter what the management said. If "they" needed to break the door down in case of emergency, then "they" could do that. He would rather pay for a damaged door than leave it virtually unlocked. His zest was catching. One by one his fellow tenants approached the management and said, in effect: "Okay, you've got the right to access. And I've got the right to safeguard myself. So I'll put on my own lock and you can break the door down if you have to. I'll take responsibility for any damage." There hasn't been an emergency or broken door to date. Again when it is necessary for building personnel to enter any apartment to make a repair or accompany an outsider (such as painter, electrician or plumber), arrangements are made ahead of time.

"Waste of time," grumbles one superintendent. "A

nuisance. My men have the right to go in any time when it fits into all the other jobs they gotta do. . . ."

But they haven't. It's *your* home. There is no reason why anyone should enter your apartment in your absence, even if you yourself have released a duplicate of your key, unless they have received your permission or are forced to do so by reason of extreme emergency. Again, check your state and local laws. Building personnel, owners, management and tenants should know that it is now illegal in some states (or counties, or cities) to enter an apartment without the tenant's permission unless there is an extreme emergency. What is an emergency? Here the superintendent, or other man in charge, must be the judge—which is one reason why you want qualified personnel to run the building. Does the superintendent have good reason to believe that a life is in danger? That property may be severely damaged if he does not act? That a burst pipe or other extreme inconvenience requires instant action? Then he has a right to think in terms of "emergency," and act accordingly.

"So, we need a key," says the grumbling superintendent. "And not one of those sealed things, either. A master key, so we can get in right away and don't waste time. What if there's a fire?"

"I was standing at this apartment door," reports another superintendent, "in the process of opening it up, when the firemen just pushed me aside and broke the door down. So what good were keys under these circumstances? A fireman is not going to use them."

Well, those are the pro's and con's, and maybe they are extremes. But a great many security-conscious people, superintendents among them, firmly believe that project and other apartment dwellers should have the right to a second lock and key. This right, they feel, should be the law of the land, because without it the tenant simply is not secure.

Until it is law, the tenant who feels he is not adequately protected because of overall security laxness (including masterkeyed or other inadequate locks) and is unable under his lease to make desired improvements, should at least do the following: Provide himself with a good, sturdy doorchain and a peephole, keyed window locks, and perhaps a folding gate at the fire escape window. Note down the serial numbers, if any, and descriptions of all valuables that he must keep in his apartment. Keep other valuables in a safe deposit box in the bank. Join with other tenants in lobbying for the right to protect himself with locks of his own choice.

The New House: Will Your Home Be Your Castle?

So you won the lottery, and now you can build your dream house. In the good old days, whenever they were, you probably wouldn't have given a thought to burglar-proofing while building, but now you might as well give it some thought even while you look for a lot.

You will, of course, be very careful about what sort of neighborhood you choose to buy into, and you will realize that your security is going to depend in part on the location of your property. For example: How far away is the nearest house? Are there any near neighbors to offer help if needed? Will they be able to hear your alarm, or your barking dog? Will they have an unobstructed view of any part of your house when it is completed, or of your projected path or driveway? Is the general area well-lit with streetlamps and lights from other homes?

What are the adjacent neighboorhoods like? Are they very prosperous, slightly seedy, distinctly shabby, over-crowded, underpopulated? Is there, nearby, an expensive shopping center, a park, a dock area, or a warehouse dis-trict? What sort of people frequent these neighborhoods, and the immediate neighborhood of your choice? No, you don't have to be a snob; you just have to weigh these things in your own mind.

Is your proposed property in a heavily wooded area? Isolated, bare, undeveloped? Set far back from the street? Squeezed between a couple of other houses? Across the street from Kelly's Shamrock Bar, or a household full of frantically energetic little children? Are you *sure* you want to build here?

All right, you want to build.

Basic Defenses

When you start from the ground up you can build in your protective measures. By selecting your builders with care and giving as much personal attention to the job as you can (in person or through your architect), you can be sure of your materials, from brick to wood to metal to glass. Door frames and doors can be as sturdy as they come. So can window frames, and roofs, and walls. An attractive outside wall, not so high as to obscure the view from or of the house, can be planned to follow or even accentuate some particularly attractive aspect of the building—unless your landscaping plans include a hedge or a picket fence covered with climbing roses. But do, if you are to have a yard or garden, include an outer barrier of some kind. It is the outer perimeter of your defense system.

You have an excellent chance, while planning your new home, to landscape your grounds in such a way as to discourage burglars. Flower beds and ornamental miniatures, for example, are better from the point of view of your security than shady nooks. It will be a while before your trees and shrubs are thick enough or tall enough to be of much help to the hopeful thief, but do bear in mind that potentially thick shrubs and tall trees will some day make good cover for an unauthorized visitor. An open sweep of lawn, exposed to the view of residents, neighbors and passersby, is enough to put off many a thief, particularly if it slopes downward to a perimeter growth of thorny hedge.

Your windows can be built so that they are literally impregnable. Ask your architect to dream up something for you. If you deal with a man of imagination and resource, you will find that burglar-resistant windows can be very attractive indeed. Large windows with small, diamond-shaped panes, for instance, are lovely looking and can be very strong. The strength is in the framing between each section of glass. It is easily possible to design even a wall-sized window, if that is your wish, that incorporates reinforced steel instead of the standard wood molding. Each small pane of plate glass is held in place with a strong little strip of its own. A burglar, on seeing this, might get the impression that he could break a few panes, snap the framing around the gaps, and crawl right through. He would be absolutely wrong. Reinforced steel strips are not toothpicks; they are highly burglar-resistant.

Then there are those attractive little windows that consist of a series of long, narrow slots, or miniature portholes, or that are set on the diagonal rather than on the straight, or executed in some other fancy or unusual design. What makes them so nice is that they can literally cover a whole wall of the house, letting in fresh air, light and breeze while at the same time offering maximum security.

As for picture windows, you can safeguard these from breakage in one of two ways. Neither way is inexpensive, but if either helps to keep burglars out then you can consider your money well spent. The first way is the use of "unbreakable" glass. There is no glass made that will resist every type of massive onslaught, but there is one that can be highly recommended today for store windows and thus for residential pictures windows as well. It is called Secur-Lite and is made by the Amerada Glass Company, a division of Globe Glass Manufacturing Company of 2001 Greenleaf

Avenue, Elk Grove Village, Illinois 60007. This glass will eventually crack when subjected to repeated forceful blows with a large hammer, brick, baseball bat, lead pipe or other heavy object, but it is protected by a special burglary-resistant glazing material that stubbornly resists a breakthrough. Its special lamination holds the glass together so that it w.ll not shatter into pieces nor fall out of place. In effect, the glass bends rather than breaks, and a breaking tool swung against it will simply bounce back. It is a fine, clear glass, appropriate for picture windows, that costs maybe twice as much as ordinary glass. However, since you probably plan on only one picture window and in all likelihood will never need to replace it, the cost isn't all that bad.

Another way to protect your picture window is to doll it up with ornamental metalwork on the outside. This can be placed far enough away from the glass to make it very awkward for anyone to attempt any action with a glass cutter or other close-up tool, and should be designed in such a manner as to make it extremely difficult for a would-be thief to crawl or even reach in after noisily shattering the glass with a thrown object. The visual effect of such a window can be extremely ornamental and attractive. The "picture" is set in a superb frame which does nothing to detract from the view and actually improves the house from the outside. Indeed, many windows can be handled in a similar way; you do not have to have a picture window to make your windows both safe and picturesque. If metalwork is your choice, consider these factors when installing it:

Some metal is soft, some is brittle. Don't get either type. Check with your builder or architect and make sure that you get good, sturdy metal that cannot be sawed through or snapped.

You will need a secondary exit in case of fire. Leave yourself with at least one window that you can use when you can't get out by door. Supply it with a keyed lock or a grating that is latched from within.

You may need to provide even your metal-ornamented windows with a keyed lock, rather than a latch, for additional security. This will depend on how much metalwork you can stand to have on your windows, how much freedom of action a burglar may have in your neighborhood in terms of time and noise, and other factors that you alone can think of.

Metalwork itself can often be set off and improved by artistic use of window plantings, flowering climbers, or

plants on window sills. By exercising some esthetic judgment, you can have the most beautiful *and* the most secure
windows in the neighborhood.

A good architect should 'be able to come up with many
other ideas for incorporating security features into your new
home. Just be sure you don't neglect the subject in your
discussions with him. And be equally sure that the builder's
work, the builder's materials and the builder's hardware
come up to your security specifications. You are not going to
permit him to install main doors with cheap knob-locks that
can be snapped off with a wrench; you are going to see that
he puts in the sturdy stuff that you ordered. Preferably, you
will personally call on a qualified locksmith to take care of
all locking installations.

While the wiring is being done and the lighting fixtures
installed, you may want to include the burglar alarm system
of your choice. It's easier at this stage than later. It is also
easy to incorporate, in your lighting plan, a system of outside lighting that will flood the outside of your house, or
your garden, with a flick of a switch or two inside the house.
You may even want to include some interior remote
switches so that you can, for instance, turn on the living
room light when you're in the bedroom, or the bedroom
light when you're in the recreation room, or the porch light
when you're in the study. (It is generally a pretty good plan
to show a light—preferably more than one—when you suspect a thief is entering or already in your home. And it is
usually wiser to show the light where you are *not* . . . in case
he happens to be spoiling for trouble.)

Some people like to incorporate what they call a safety
room into their home planning. This isn't much of an oper-

ation, and can easily be done after the house is built, but it isn't a bad idea to consider it from the start.

The Safety Room

Understandably, a lot of householders feel that having a safety room is carrying security-consciousness a little too far. Others, however, have reason to be grateful for having provided themselves and their families with a retreat from unbalanced intruders who have shown that they would as soon confront their victims as run from them.

The safety room doesn't have to be a vault. In appearance, it is just another comfortable room in daily use. Often it is the main, or master, bedroom. Whatever the room chosen, it should have one doorway that is quickly accessible to the whole family, and at least one window through which escape is possible. Walls should not be of the partition type, but solid.

The door must be of thick, high-quality hardwood set securely into a sturdy frame. Hinges should be mounted inside, pins included, and secured with long, strong screws. The lock side of the door should be equipped with a good pin tumbler cylinder that operates a heavy deadbolt, plus a barrel bolt or doorchain. Windows should be guarded with metal gates secured and operated from the inside. The room should be large enough so that no one has to cower near or in line with the door. (Desperadoes have been known to shoot through doors that otherwise defeat them.)

Further, the room should be equipped with a telephone. The local precinct number and the police emergency number, if any, must be on prominent and permanent display. It is also advisable to have on hand a small, portable alarm and an extra light source, in case the intruder decides to go around cutting wires. The light source can be a battery-powered table lamp or flashlight; the alarm may be one of those little hand-sized devices that cost so little yet—if you choose the right one—let out such an ear-splitting blast. These can be purchased in most dime or hardware stores. Since they do not depend on the house wiring, they cannot be deactivated by the most skillful of thieves. Batteries for both flashlight and alarm should be regularly checked.

The safety room is only a standby. It should never be relied upon in place of overall security precautions. It is far better to protect your whole house than permit yourself and your family to be boxed into one room—supposing, that is, that you can all get there in time.

The Ready-to-wear House: Alterations At Small Additional Charge

What to do with the aging house you've decided to move into? Or the one you're already in, that suddenly strikes you as being about as solid as a slice of Swiss cheese?

There's plenty you can do with it, and plenty of wide-ranging precautions you can take.

Perimeter Defenses

The farthest out of all your defenses may sometimes be the best. It comes in two overlapping parts.

The first part consists of immediately becoming part of, or helping to form, a community or block association devoted to the protection and betterment of the neighborhood. This can be done with the help of your city councilman, local precinct, or any interested local civic group. Indeed, it can be done by you and your neighboring citizens without any help, but you had best inform the police of what you are doing and generally make your intentions public or run the risk of being suspected of evil doings or at least of vigilante activities.

The purpose of your association is to establish a pool of information regarding the proper use of locks, alarms, lights and other safeguards around all your homes; to inculcate in youngsters, and all members of the family, the need to use such safeguards; to patrol, in turn, the block or blocks included within the perimeters of the neighborhood selected; and to be on call, in turn, to answer requests for help.

There are many such neighborhood associations already in existence, some established with and some without the cooperation of the local police. Even where the police have not served as active planners they have been kept informed, and in most cases they freely admit to having benefited by the work of the community association. It takes a little—just a little—of the load off them.

The second part of your far-out defense is, simply, to be a good neighbor, whether or not you are part of a neighborhood protective group. Get involved. That doesn't mean you are to snoop. It means that you should get to know your neighbors just well enough to help them in time of need and have them do the same for you. It means offering to keep an eye on another family's home when they're away, collect their mail, pick up the circulars, and maybe even cut the grass. It means being concerned when you see anyone suspicious or notice any furtive activity near their home whether they are in it or not, and calling the police or taking personal action consistent with your own safety (turning on enough lights to flood the neighboring yard, setting off your own local alarm, strolling past with your dog, blowing a shrill whistle, or shouting out loud from a safe distance) to scare off an intruder and get help.

In neighborhoods where people do get involved, and especially in neighborhoods that have their own police-recognized patrols, the crime rate tends to drop perceptibly. Word does get around. The cagey criminal prefers to stay away from potential danger zones.

Outer Physical Barriers

Your other effective outer defenses are the barriers you set up around the borders of your property. If you have a yard that can be fenced, walled or hedged, then by all means use such a barrier. Even a low wall with a gate can be something of a deterrent, so long as it is not so low that it can easily be stepped over. Hoisting himself over any sort of hurdle, especially under the light of a streetlamp, is not the burglar's favorite activity.

And how about attaching a small local alarm to the gate, and activating it at night just before retiring? It may be a very simple one, but once it goes off our thief is unlikely to spend too much time trying to locate it.

A chain link fence with a lockable gate is effective around some large properties. It is not the most beautiful thing in the world, but it can be dressed up with climbing vines. More attractive is a wrought-iron fence or a wooden picket fence. These are not difficult to surmount, but if they are tall enough they can be awkward for the would-be thief. At least they are a psychological deterrent, something to give him pause. The same is true of a woven wire fence or a thick hedge. Whatever your preference, bear in mind that *no* obstacle you place around your house should be dangerous or hurtful. If a neighborhood child should be attracted by the barrier (for the thrill of climbing it or showing off) and then cut by broken glass or stabbed by metal spikes or shocked by even the mildest electrical charge, you might find yourself in trouble. Under certain circumstances you can even be in trouble if your barrier harms an adult, trespasser though he may be. And in some states it is illegal to use such deterrents as jagged glass or spikes. So be sure to check local statutes before investing in any barrier that the law considers potentially dangerous or definitely taboo.

Possibly your best bet in barriers is a combination of hedge and fence. The hedge should be wide rather than high, and of the prickly or thorny variety. Thorns are more of a discomfort than a hazard, but the discomfort can be considerable. The fence should be placed outside the hedge, partly to protect inquisitive little fingers from getting scratched and partly to make things more difficult for a hedge-jumping thief (may he land in the middle!). Such a fence, which should be just high enough to prevent a tall intruder from stepping over it, might either be of the chain link type or of woven wire with no protruding sharp ends. With the fence on the outside and the prickly hedge on the inside, you can be fairly sure that most burglars will think twice about braving your barrier. And if the gate has an alarm attachment . . . he might think three times, and go away.

Lighting

It is law, in some parts of this country, for multiple dwellings, apartment houses, hotels, rooming houses and so on to keep a strong outside light burning throughout the night. In many areas the law demands that business establishments do the same, or at least have interior lights that spill out to flood the street outside. In a few places such a law covers private homes as well. This is a good law; this is an excellent law. A street that is splashed with light from every building on it is a street that the burglar does not like. Thus, even where such lighting is not required, the wise homeowner or landlord or business proprietor will provide his own illumination.

Every home should have an outside light fixture to provide bright, nightlong illumination for the front door and its immediate surroundings. This should be used every night, turned on by the householder when he is there and by timer when he is not. In this way, each resident of the block contributes not only to his own security but to the security of the entire block. Additionally, one inside light kept burning all night long and muted by a drawn shade is something of a puzzle to the burglar. Is somebody up? Somebody in but asleep? Everybody out, and faking it? He doesn't know the answer.

Some houses and their surrounding grounds need additional outside lights. These considerations seldom affect city folk or dwellers in semidetached or barely detached houses, but some suburban homes with spreads of tree-shaded lawn and high flower beds and shrubs do have need of them. When the inside lights are turned out, the sides and back of the house are often in almost total darkness. Or the edge of the front garden, if not lit by a street lamp or reached by the front door light, may be in heavy shadow. Spotlights or floodlights, according to individual needs, may be used to fill in the dark places.

If you have a shadowy garden you can easily mount one or more such lights on a post at some distance from your house so that it, or they, flood(s) the border of your garden and any shrubbery that offers concealment. Or you can mount the lights on the post or on the house itself so that they illuminate the otherwise dark corners of the house. Or you may have a combination of such lights, so that the dark corners of both house and garden can be lit at the same time. You will of course take care, in mounting them, to set them up in such a way that they do not shine in through your own windows or the windows of your neighbors. You don't want to be blinded by them when you look outside, and you don't want to be the neighborhood pest.

One lighting expert has this to offer: "If it's a suburban home with a fair amount of property, I recommend two sets of lights. These may be either floods or spots, depending on just what you want to light and how you want the place to look. Put one set as far away from the house as you can get them and aim them so that they fall directly on the dark areas of the house. Then mount another set of lights, preferably floods, on the outside of the house where they're going to be most handy to you at night. Your first set of lights is going to make the burglar see his own shadow when he moves toward the house—and it'll be a massive one. He's going to think that everybody in the neighborhood sees it, too, and this is a great psychological deterrent. Your second set of lights will light him up like Christmas when he crosses the yard. Use one and then the other—and then you'll really have him pinned to the board, trapped between the lights."

But you really don't need to go this far. Just use enough light so that he doesn't want to cross your yard at all, and you're in business.

Now suppose that you have provided yourself with good perimeter defenses, from neighborhood patrol to fences to gate-alarm to lights. Our burglar may manage to find his way through all of them. Or suppose that, because of the nature of your property, you have been unable to install any of them with the exception of a couple of lights. With or without adequate perimeter defenses, you must concentrate on protecting the main points of entry into your house: your doors and windows.

New house or old, apartment or brownstone, cottage or mansion. . . . Whatever you live in, wherever you live, your most basic defense measures must be concentrated on the entrypoints into your home.

CHAPTER SIX

WHAT TO DO WITH THE DOORS

In any group of people, very few are going to find that their security needs, their personal preferences and their financial resources are exactly alike. Each reader must apply his own knowledge of his own needs and resources to the selection of appropriate security devices. In this he will be considerably aided by the type of qualified locksmith we discussed in an earlier chapter. The project need not be a major undertaking. Any good locksmith—especially if he realizes that you know what you are talking about—is perfectly capable of asking a few pertinent questions and advising you over the telephone, or in his shop, what is most suitable for you. It is not necessary for him to make a survey of your house, though he will do so if that is your wish. It is up to you to be able to describe every door and window in order to discuss your requirements with him. You can install your locks yourself, if you have that particular talent, or he will come to your home and do it for you.

This, then, is your first step: Make your own security survey of your home and decide in general terms at least, what must be done. Don't be like so many people and concentrate all your fire on the hardware for the front door. Know the strengths and the weaknesses of the door itself. Don't underestimate the need to secure the back door, or the side door, or the porch door, or the garage door, or the French doors, or the sliding doors . . . or any other doors. It is amazing how many people put a fine lock on the front door and flimsy locks on the others, or how many don't seem to care if the back door is crumbling off its hinges so long as the front door looks good.

Doors and Frames

Doors can be vulnerable not only in the area of the lock and hinges but in their essential makeup. Flush doors without panels are your best bet. And although a sturdy, well-constructed hardwood door, solid all the way through, is a pretty good door to have, it loses some of its value if the frame is of lesser quality or does not offer a snug fit. You will recall that an auto jack can stretch a poor frame; and also that, if there is too much air between door and frame, it is not difficult for a thief to take advantage of that space. If your frame is unsatisfactory, it is best for you to replace it or add gap-filling reinforcements in the shape of wood or metal strips. If this, for some reason, is impossible, you need a special kind of lock. Indeed, with any wooden frame, you would do well to use this special lock.

This is the "police" lock, of which there are several kinds. The principle of all is a bar or brace rather than, simply, the standard bolt, installed in such a manner as to take the stress off the doorframe and transfer it either to the door jambs (in one case) or to the floor. Your choice depends in part on your own convenience, in part on your esthetic preference, and in part on whether you have an inswinging or an outswinging door. These locks are made by two companies, Fox and Magic-Eye, and will be described in greater detail under the heading of *Door Locks*.

For this type of lock you must have sturdy doors or else get them reinforced, otherwise the frustrated thief might attempt to saw or break his way in through the center of the door. Usually, with a wooden frame, you do not have that solid hardwood door mentioned above, but rather a flimsy door that often consists only of thin wooden panels or even glass panels. If the house is not your own and you are stuck with those panels, you will have to make the best of the situation and get yourself a good double-cylinder lock (that is, one that is keyed from inside as well as outside) so that, even if the door is broken, it can't be unlocked from the inside by a groping hand. But if your home is your own, or if you can get away with a little improvement without your landlord objecting, you should by all means reinforce your glass-paneled or other inadequate door.

To reinforce a glass-paneled door, you can cover it with wire screens, bars, a sheet of heavy aluminum or a piece of plywood—and then add your double-cylinder lock for extra insurance.

If your door is the lightweight wood-panel type that consists of little more than thin plywood or veneer, or a couple of panels of thin, soft metal, you can protect it in one of the following ways:

1. Add a piece of sheet steel to the door, covering its length and width. Be sure, first, that the hinges will be able to stand the weight. They should be strong, sturdy hinges, and there should be three of them.

2. Cover the entire inside surface with a sheet of tin—

again, only if the hinges can stand the weight.

3. Add a door-sized plate of heavy-gauge aluminum. (This is not always easy to get. Look in your classified directory under Locksmiths or Metalworkers.)

4. Cover your door with a reinforcing sheet of plywood. This may very will be your best bet. It is light, neat, strong, and better looking than old paneling. Reinforcing with plywood is a simple and inexpensive way of strengthening your old door and dressing it up to look like a flush door. As any burglar knows, a flush door is much harder to break into than any sort of paneled door.

Note: When installing any such reinforcement sheets, be sure to use either carriage bolts or nonretractable screws.

If you have your choice of putting in a new door altogether, you will find that some builders and locksmiths advocate a thick hardwood door from an inch and a half to three inches thick. Other experts—locksmiths in particular—show a distinct preference for metal doors consisting of two thick, sturdy metal panels packed with sound insulating material. Both schools of thought agree that thinly paneled or veneered doors should only be used as interior doors; that is, in cases where privacy is more important than security. Perhaps surprisingly, not all experts are united against glass paneling. Those in favor reason that plate glass is quite strong, that to break it is usually a noisy business, and that such breakage can be counteracted by use of the double-cylinder lock.

All doors should be installed so that the hinges are inaccessible from the outside. Screws must be long, strong, and made of rust-proof steel, screwed deeply into door and doorframe material of high quality and good condition. After installation they should be checked every once in a while to be sure that they show no signs of loosening up or even pulling free. If in renting your home you acquire a back (or other) door with its screws and the screwholes slightly damaged, make repairs as quickly as possible. Take the screws out, remove the hinge plates and either replace them or drill new holes in them, fill in the old screwholes, and put in new—and better screws.

Should you chance to inherit a door with the hinge pins located on the outside, you must make a point of doing everything possible to ensure that the hinge side of your door is not vulnerable. If the old hinges have removable pins, replace them with new hinges that have nonremovable pins. A further precaution you can take to prevent anyone from lifting the door out at the hinge side is to incorporate a feature commonly used in safes as a real thief-baffler: Set 2 or 3 half-inch pins into the edge of the door on the hinge side—one near the top, one near the bottom, and perhaps one in the middle—and drill corresponding receiving holes into the frame. When the door is closed the pins fit into the holes to act as dowels and protect the hinge side of the door from the hinge-tamperer. Even if the thief does' succeed in removing the hinge pins, he will not be able to pull the door away from the frame.

Once in a while you will encounter surface-mounted hinges on, for instance, cellar doors. If it is not necessary to replace the old hinge, at least replace the old screws with one-way, nonretractable screws. These are special screws that can be turned clockwise only, so that you can screw them in but not out. This is not to say that they are impossible to remove by one means or another; but they are very, very difficult to get out even if you have the time, the knowledge, the tools, and a legitimate purpose in removing them. One tends to start to swear after a while.

Remember these screws when you're putting any hardware at all on the outside of your doors. It is true that most door hardware can be affixed from the inside, or at least into the edges, of door and frame, but many old-fashioned or inexpensive installations still have exposed screws in the escutcheon plate or doorknob base. These should be replaced. Also, oddly enough, people who take the trouble to install heavy, high-quality padlocks on cellar doors, garages, sheds and barns often forget all about the vulnerability of screws and leave those easily-turnable heads exposed to view. Whenever screws must be used on the outside—and excuses for this are getting fewer and fewer—they *must* be of the nonretractable variety.

If you have a transom over any door, either seal it up permanently or put a strong metal grating over it so that you can open it once in a while and get in some air. If you live in an apartment you might just as well seal it; it doesn't really let in as much air as it does pollution and noise, and it *is* quite vulnerable.

Semi-Doors

Glass-louvered doors, French doors, sliding doors and terrace doors with windows should all be protected by good, strong jimmy-proof deadlocks. These locks should, preferably, be such that they can be opened only from the inside and then only with a key; or they should be dual-cylindered. You will of course keep your key well out of reach of a grasping hand.

Sliding doors, of glass or wood, can actually be reasonably well protected in another very simple way. When they are closed they leave a channel free for you to block with a heavy curtain rod or broomstick of appropriate length. This acts as a brace, and leaves most burglars baffled. But there are good locks for sliding doors available, and even if you have a curtain rod to spare you will want to back it up with good hardware.

Interviewers, Bolts and Chains

If you have a glass-paneled exterior door, front or rear, you already have a sort of built-in interviewer. However, it is not effective if the panes are frosted, so that you can't see out, nor is it adequate if it is clear from both sides, so that you can be seen from outside. One possible solution is to replace the panes or panel with one-way glass, so that you can look out but an outsider can't see in.

Better than this is the peephole, or door interviewer, which should be used on both front and back doors. Some peepholes are no more than tiny little windows that you can open and peek through. These are far from the best that you can get, for they are not so tiny that someone standing outside can't jab in a finger or a screwdriver or a knife or a gun—and thrust it right into your face. Also, most of the large ones are quite easy to open or break from the outside, permitting the entry of a length of stiff wire or something similar that can be manipulated in such a way 'as to slide back your door chain or twist the thumbturn of your lock or otherwise interfere with your locking system.

A small glass viewer is slightly better. In this case, one-way glass is not highly recommended, nor is plain glass. The drawbacks of such viewers are that they are just small enough so that you have to get pretty close to be able to peer through them, at which point your eyeball is visible from outside even if the glass is supposedly one-way; just large enough—and the glass thin enough—to permit something sharp and strong to be stuck through, possibly into your eye; just designed so that your field of vision is limited to what is directly in line with the hole.

Sal Schillizzi is very strong on the door interviewer with the smallest possible hole. If such an inteviewer is forced off the door, the burglar cannot manipulate through the hole. "I'm very much against the one-way mirror glass, or any single-glass peephole. If you have your eye right up against it, you can get broken glass in your eye, or even get something squirted in. Anyway, one-way glass gives you limited, very limited, vision. The double-glass, wide-angled lens will give you a good view and better eye protection."

The best type of viewer—no matter what its frame or what it may look like from the outside—consists of a powerful little lens made of two layers of thick glass set inside a tiny, narrow tube. Possibly the finest of such lenses is the microviewer ("Le Microviseur") made by Bloscop of France. It measures about two-tenths of an inch in diameter and offers an incredibly wide-angled view. You may not be able to find this particular little lens just everywhere (in fact, you may have to import it), but you should be able to find something similar through your locksmith.

You will have to shop around to find a good one. Look through several of them to compare distortion and viewing angle. You will want to get as wide-angled a view as you can without sacrificing clarity. Some of the cheaper viewers will appear, at first glance, to satisfy your requirements. Look at them again, closely, and make sure that the "glass" is not plastic. Plastic scratches very easily, and a scratched lens makes viewing difficult. The best of the wide-angled glass lenses offer a slightly distorted (curved) but nevertheless sharp picture of the area to either side of your door as well as straight ahead. This means that anyone trying to duck out of sight will have to get well away from your door before he is out of viewing range. The glass area, furthermore, is so tiny that only the smallest of instruments can be used to spike through it—which in itself is not too easy to do because of the two separate glass layers.*

A barrel bolt is some people's idea of a good, solid, if old-fashioned piece of auxiliary hardware. It does have its points as an extra device for bolting yourself in, but it does not have the value of a doorchain and should not be used instead of a chain.

The chief value, and purpose, of a doorchain is that it permits you, after peeking at your caller through the inter-

---

* Consultant locksmith Schillizzi has devised a peephole cylinder lock that incorporates the little French lens right into the lock cylinder. Unless you happen to be a child you have to stoop to peer through it, but this in itself is advantageous. In the first place, it's good for a child to be able to see who is at the door; in the second, nobody expects to be peeked at through a pin tumbler lock. Set in the cylinder, the lens doesn't even look like a peephole. From the outside it looks as though it might be an electric eye, possibly part of an alarm system, and this in itself could be enough to change the mind of a would-be peephole-prodder. S.S. calls his invention the See-Through Lock.

viewer, to open the door just wide enough to query him and receive the telegram or whatever it is. Obviously you cannot do this with a barrel bolt. There are many chains on the market. The cheaper ones are quite flimsy and can be snapped with a little effort. Also, the screws that are supplied with them are likely to be short. If these are screwed into wood that is a little on the soft side, they can be yanked out with ease. All it takes is one sudden push against a partly open door from the outside. What you need is a chain that is smash-proof and hack-proof, and comes supplied with long, strong screws. Segal is one lock company that makes the finest in doorchains. They use a bicycle or motorcycle type of chain that is very tough indeed.

It is possible to purchase chains that are lockable by key, permitting the householder to lock the chain into place from the outside when leaving his home. This would seem to be a very good idea, but regrettably the locks that are being used on this chain-lock device are pitifully easy to pick. So, until better such devices are made, you would be well-advised to get a good, bicycle-type chain for use while you are at home and separate locks for general door security.

When installing your doorchain you want to be sure that you place it in such a way that, when it is engaged, it permits the door to open no more than two inches and preferably less. Contrary to some things you read about chain installation, the slide portion *should* be horizontal, not vertical or heavily slanting. At most, there can be a very slight slant down toward the edge of the door. Your purpose is to install the device securely and make the opening narrow. If it is wider than the specified two inches, all sorts of things can come in . . . including clutching hands and manipulating devices.

Totally different types of door-restraining devices are available and preferred by some people. One is intended to serve the purpose of a doorchain and, in a sense, double as a brace lock; but it isn't on the door, it hasn't got a chain, and it isn't really a lock. It is actually a little springloaded doorstop or shaft that pops up from the floor just inside the doorway. Less visible than a doorchain, it is installed in the floor and remains flush with it until a touch of the foot causes it to rise. In its erect position it permits the door to open no more than two inches. When not needed it can be depressed into the floor with another touch of the foot. Not all locksmiths are particularly enthusiastic about this little device, even though its manufacturers regard it as tamper-proof. It is not actually tamper-proof, because a suitably shaped object may be inserted around the edge of the slightly open door, or in the narrow crack between door and floor, to depress the little shaft. Nor is it completely foolproof. Neglect in periodically making sure that there is no dirt in the receptacle, or carelessness in pushing. it down before going out, may let the doorstop pop up minutes later to lock out not only the thief but the rightful resident. Still, few things are perfect, and this is not a bad little gadget at all when installed correctly and used with care.

Yet another such deviec is the Racine notched-type door guard, which is recommended by many locksmiths. It locks the door ajar in any one of three positions, and defies manipulation. Of all door guards, it is the only one that offers any sort of real protection in the open position, and the only one that offers any versatility. You can still use the narrow opening when receiving a stranger; but you can safely use the wide one when airing out the house.

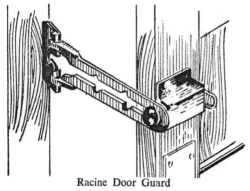

Racine Door Guard

Keys and Common Sense

When you get your new locks you will be getting new keys. You might just as well decide how you're going to keep control of them before you get them. Many people hand keys out indiscriminately to friends, relatives, and household help. This sometimes proves to be an error. A set for each responsible member of the family, and a spare set to turn over to one responsible friend or relative in case of emergency, should be quite enough.

House keys must be kept separate from car keys. If they are left in the car at a parking lot they may just possibly tempt parking lot attendants or their associates, or parking lot prowlers—of which there are many. It sometimes happens that a careless person leaves all his keys in his car, along with identification or correspondence that gives away his name and address. This gives the opportunistic thief an open invitation to drive away in the car and rob the house. In fact, this has been done successfully on a number of occasions. If there is anyone home, the man (usually a doorbell ringer) has a ready story and makes a swift departure; if there isn't he goes in. It is not surprising that even watchful neighbors fail to become suspicious. A familiar car drives up, a man gets out—for all anyone knows, a close friend or maybe brother to the householder—opens the door with a key, and emerges some time later to drive off with a few packages. It all looks very normal, until the losses are discovered. Sometimes such a thief returns the car and sometimes he does not. On occasion it is convenient for him just to borrow it and take it back to where he found it, so that he can use the facilities of that same parking lot again. After all, he can pick up a car any time he wants one.

Key cases or key rings should be marked in such a way that the owner can be tracked down through the telephone book or other reference source. Least of all should they bear the owner's address. They can, however, bear a single distinctive mark or initial for descriptive purposes.

If you should happen to lose keys that are unmarked except for that one private little symbol, you run very little danger of having your locks compromised. However, if you chase around all over the place asking for them, you immediately identify yourself as their owner. If the wrong person finds or has already found them he will waste no time in discovering where you live and what locks are fitted for these keys. What to do about this possibility? Be crafty! Send a friend around asking for your keys. Fool the would-be thief. If he decides to use the found keys, or makes copies before returning the originals to the man who claims to be their owner, your locks will not be vulnerable . . . and neither will your friend's. There stands the frustrated thief, with egg on his face and a handful of keys for which he cannot find the locks.

If you do happen to lose keys that are in any way identifiable by anyone outside your immediate, trusted circle, you should change your locks immediately. That is, change the cylinders for new ones or have your existing tumblers reset; preferably the former. It is also wise to change your lock cylinders if you have been obliged to part with unsatisfactory domestic help. This is by no means to suggest that your ex-employee is necessarily dishonest, but if you have any reason to suspect that he or she may bear a grudge or harbor any designs on your possessions you may as well take that simple precaution. It is not unheard of for a dissatisfied employee to keep a legitimately obtained key or make a copy before returning it.

Businessmen as well as householders should exercise discretion when handing out keys to their premises. They, too, should be aware of the possibility that a resentful or dishonest ex-employee may some day return with a duplicate key, and should take steps to forestall such entry.

Women in particular often need to be reminded to be more careful with their keys. Miss Stern, for instance, is expecting her parents for dinner at her apartment when she suddenly realizes that she's out of salad dressing. Out she runs, leaving her key under the doormat, where she knows they'll think of looking if she's not back by the time they arrive. Only trouble is, the old folks aren't the only people who might think of looking there. Miss Espeland is a little cagier: she leaves *her* key under her neighbor's mat. Miss Kennard is taller; she puts her key on the narrow ledge above her door. Mrs. Moore is expecting her grown children and their children for the long weekend. She's not quite sure what time they're arriving and she still hasn't done all her shopping, so she attaches a note to the door which reads, "Darlings, the key is in the usual place." Now *that* poses a little puzzle, but only a little one. Burglars know all the usual places and some unusual ones as well. It doesn't take them long to complete an efficient search.

Sometimes they don't have to search at all. If a casual loiterer watches Mrs. Cornish tuck something under the third flower pot from the left and then drive away in her car, he might as well be tempted to stroll over and take a look under that flower pot.

Not all keys left lying around in such a manner are used by the criminal the moment he locates them. He may prefer to choose his own time for making an entry. He might simply keep the key for later use, relying on the fact that many a householder cannot be bothered to change a lock after "mislaying" a key; or he might, if he is reasonably well-organized, be equipped with the simple makings for taking an impression of that key, after which he will return at his own convenience with his very own custom-made duplicate.

Door Locks

Those whose business is to work with locks and keys of all varieties, including locking devices for petty cash boxes, cabinets, mailboxes, slot machines and so on as well as doors and windows, generally divide key locks into four general categories: warded locks, lever tumbler locks, disk tumbler locks, and pin tumbler locks. They are faced, today, with the problem of categorizing an interesting miscellany that defies definition because it includes mechanisms that cannot be described as "key locks" and others based on unusual tumbler systems. In the meantime we will lump them all into a fifth category and deal with them in detail when we come to them.

The first three types are not, and for the most part should not be, used as exterior locks and require only brief discussion.

The warded lock is the simplest of all locks and offers the least security. It yields easily to the crudest of pass keys. The cheapest padlocks are warded locks; you wouldn't want to hang such a padlock on any outer door. The only legitimate use of a warded lock is to keep the kids out of the closets or the camphor chest.

Lever tumbler locks serve a variety of purposes. They are seldom used on exterior doors in the United States, although they are still widely used in Europe. The good ones offer excellent security and two drawbacks: high price, and an oversized key. So good are the highest-quality lever locks that varieties of them are used on floor safes, safe deposit boxes—and even in jails. Others of lesser quality, which are the ones we usually see, are used to secure desk drawers, mail boxes, lockers and the like.

The disk or wafer tumbler lock is generally used on cabinets, desks and a variety of low-security receptacles. It is also to be found on automobiles. This type of lock offers more security than the warded lock, but that is about all that can be said for it—except for one so-called disk tumbler lock that is in a class of its own by virtue of its unique design and operating mechanism.

The pin tumbler lock, described earlier, is the only one of the four main lock categories that serves as a good exterior lock. It is widely accepted and used as such. In fact, it is such a versatile lock that it is now being used in some cases to secure automobiles, motorcycles, money chests, and anything else to which man's ingenuity can adapt it. The simplest of these locks yield fairly readily to a good pickman. Others are superb.

The fifth—the miscellaneous—category includes locks that do not depend on springs and standard pins. One such is based on rotating detainer disks, another is magnetic, others are keyless, and yet another is a total lock unit that employs a variety of fairly standard components in a unique combination. Some of these locks are excellent, more than worthy rivals to the pin tumbler lock; others are still in the experimental stage and are thought by some locksmiths to be little more than gimmicks.

From here on we will disregard the first three categories and concentrate on the last two. In doing so we take note of the fact that a lock, by definition, is a "fastening," and because what we really want to know is how to fasten our doors, we have to set up a more practical way to categorize exterior door locks. From the consumer's point of view there are four basic types:

1. *The springlatch lock, or snaplock.* This simple fastening is the one often referred to as a nightlatch (not to be confused with nightstop), although no one in possession of his faculties or the facts would rely on this one either night or day. It is tapered or beveled in shape so that it will snap automatically into the lock strike when you close your door. Convenient for the lazy man, it is also convenient for the burglar with his little loid. This is the cheapest of all locks and, by a long way, the least effective. It should be used only as a primary or convenience lock and must be supplemented with a good secondary lock.

The simplest of these springlatch locks are absolutely useless, except maybe for holding the door closed against a breeze. The better ones do offer a degree of security—they "deadlatch" when snapped into place. There are several varieties of this better type. One consists of a spring bolt protected by a small device which automatically "kills" the spring when the door is pulled shut, so that the latch cannot be slid out of place; one employs a half-round trigger bolt that serves the same purpose; another is equipped with a trigger guard that actually blocks the latch so that, again, it cannot be shimmed out of the lock strike. The drawback of all such latches, ingenious though they may be, is that the tongue is very short. Unless the door fits very precisely into its frame, a jimmy can be used to widen the gap at the lock area and pop the latch right out of the strike socket.

It is possible to improve the situation somewhat and protect the latch by installing a metal bracket with a flange, or a piece of angle iron, to cover that vulnerable slot between door and frame. However, while this will protect the latch from the loid, it may not offer total security against the jimmy. *Or* against the pick; the lock cylinders of these simple latches are very easy to pick. In sum, the lesson is: Even a deadlatching springlatch should not be used as a main lock.

However, there is one really good latch lock of this approximate type that breaks all the rules. Its latch deadlocks automatically when the door is closed; it has a small secondary latch which, when activated, causes an untapered rim to extend around the main latch, not only making it longer but rendering it shimproof; and it has an excellent cylinder. This is the Abloy lock, made in Finland but purchasable in the United States and Canada. What's more, the Abloy company breaks another rule with another of its locks. The latter has a *square* bolt that automatically springs into the lock strike with the slamming of the door.

2. *The square deadbolt.* This is a sturdy, unbeveled bolt that is activated only (if it isn't an Abloy) when you double-lock your door with either a key or a thumbturn. It gives better protection than the springlatch. Because it is unbeveled it cannot be shimmed, and because it is longer than the springlatch it offers just that much more resistance to jimmying. However, it is far from being jimmy-proof. This type of bolt, with its accompanying lock mechanism, is made by just about every lock manufacturer in existence. Cylinder quality varies, but that need not be much of a factor because you can nearly always substitute a better one.

3. *The jimmy-proof deadlock.* This lock has two vertical deadbolts that lock into sturdy metal eyes (which constitute the strike) set onto the door jamb. This means that the door is actually clamped to the jamb just as securely on the lock side as on the hinge side—possibly even more securely. The prototype of this lock was, and is, made by Segal. Others of the type are now being manufactured by several companies. Not all of these imitations, or variations, match the quality of the Segal. The latter, finest of the jimmy-proof deadlocks, can only be jimmied with extreme force, such as that applied by a fireman with a heavy-duty crowbar. Even then it is seldom that the lock itself actually breaks; what is more likely to happen is that the lock strike is violently wrenched off the frame. Successful stretching by means of an auto jack or other device is also extremely rare. Again, it is the jamb and not the lock that gives, leaving unmistakable evidence of forcible entry.

The one drawback to the fine Segal lock is that its cylinder is standard and fairly easy to pick. But this is not a major drawback; you can replace that cylinder with one that is pick-resistant or even pick-proof.

4. *The bar-type lock.* Locks of this type are actually jimmy-proof, so that in a sense they belong in the previous

category, but because of their special characteristics they demand special attention. The Fox Police Lock Company, for one, makes a type of lock that completely does away with the standard bolt. One variety, the brace bar lock, is designed for use on an in-swinging door. Instead of a locking bolt that enters the doorframe it has a heavy steel brace bar that locks the door to the floor. The top end of the (removable) bar slots into a receptacle on the door, and the bottom end fits into a metal socket that is recessed into the floor. The lock is made to operate from the outside. It is equipped with a good pin tumbler cylinder which can, if it makes you feel yet more secure, be replaced with a more highly pick-resistant cylinder.

The second variety of Fox lock, primarily used for stores, storage rooms, warehouses, stock rooms and the like, may be used on doors swinging in either direction but is particularly recommended for use on doors that swing outward. This is known as the double bolt or double bar lock. It consists of a pair of bolt bars reaching horizontally across the door from a central latchset and extending deep into the casings or door jambs. This, in effect, actually locks the door *behind* its frame.

What many locksmiths regard as an advance on the original police locks is the type made by Magic Eye. There are two varieties, the best of which employs an outsized, side-looking deadbolt of incredible sturdiness as well as the floor-locking brace bar. With this heavy-duty lock, as with the other police locks, you must have a basically strong or reinforced door.

These, then, are the basic types of locks available. Your choice of lock is going to depend on a number of factors: Whether you are looking for a primary or secondary lock. What kind of door you have. What you like the looks of and can best live with. How much you can spend. The quality of the cylinder that comes with the lock. The adaptability of the lock to other cylinders. The type of home you have. And—on how important it is to you to provide your home with overall, maximum security.

The police officials, when asked their recommendations for door hardware, are in wide agreement that all entrance doors should be equipped with a primary or convenience lock, a sturdy secondary lock that is both jimmy-proof and pick-resistant, a chainbolt, and a peephole. The primary lock, they suggest, should be of the springlatch variety with a built-in deadlocking feature; that is, the latch should automatically deadlock when the door is slammed. This lock must be equipped with a pin tumbler cylinder of at least standard quality. The secondary, or real lockout, burglar-bamboozling lock should be of the drop-bolt variety (Segal-type, although the police are quite scrupulous about avoiding brand names), preferably keyed from within as well as without, and thus dual-cylindered. The outer cylinder should be pick-resistant; and the lock should be mounted with one-way screws. Further, it should be fitted with a nightstop or lockout button which, when activated from inside, will prevent anyone from entering even if they do have the proper key. (This is supposed to be a defense against the would-be thief who has somehow obtained possession of your key. The fact that it can also be used by wife against husband or husband against wife is not ordinarily the concern of the police.) There are times, however, when you should not install that little lockout button. It can be a great nuisance to you if you happen to have a large playful dog or a small playful child. If you should ever be obliged to leave one or the other locked in and even momentarily unsupervised, you might wind up breaking the door down. Either large dog or playful child could conceivably push that little knob by accident—and lock you out. This happens very rarely, but once per person is enough.

So much for general recommendations. Now for specifics.

CHAPTER SEVEN

WHEN TO USE WHAT

The nature of your door is of considerable importance in the selection of your main, or security, lock. It is less important, however, in your choice of a primary, or convenience, lock. There are many of the latter available on the market at reasonable cost.

Primary Locks

There are essentially two types of primary locks. One is the standard mortise lock (recessed into the door), consisting of a springlatch and a deadbolt. The other is the key-in-the-knob lock. Many doors, you will find, "come with" the mortise type. If you have a choice, don't settle for it; if you can change it, do that.

The mortise type of primary lock presents a number of drawbacks. In most cases, a mortise lock can be shimmed if you neglect to double-lock it, which is not true of the key-in-the-knob lock. Also, in most cases, the set-screw can be loosened if a would-be thief is given a brief opportunity at an open door. This tampering is impossible with the key-in-the-knob lock. Replacement of a mortise lock is difficult, because mortise locks are not standard in size. Further, on a door opening outward, the pushbuttons of most mortise locks can be manipulated by thin wire from the outside. And in some cases, the knob of the mortise lock can be removed so that the lock can be manipulated through the hubs.

This is not to say that all key-in-the-knob locks are altogether free of the faults of the mortise lock. Quality variations are tremendous. The cheapest ones are practically useless. Some are so feebly made and of such inferior metal (zinc-type metal, for instance) that they can be snapped off when a little extra strength is exerted—either by accident or design. The better ones are quite sturdy and are equipped with an automatic deadlocking latch. Some are available in good, pressed steel. Careful shopping around will get you a really good product.

The great advantage of key-in-the-knob locks is that they are standard in size. Thus, if you already have one and want to replace it for any reason, you can easily do so without cutting into your door and making new holes in it. Even the good key-in-the-knob locks can be damaged under what we might call semicontrolled conditions. While a poor one will give easily under burglarious assault or even your own excessive haste and carelessness in wrenching the door open, a better one may suffer when the movers come in with the heavy furniture. If they should hit the lock with the solid oak dining room table for example, they will probably damage it. When this happens it is to your advantage to be able to replace the lock as quickly as possible without having to hack up your door.

Most lock manufacturers make key-in-the-knob locks.

Schlage Key-in-Knob Lock

Schlage has some excellent ones, both of the standard and heavy-duty variety. Other fine ones are made by Arrow, Yale, Corbin and Weiser. Of course, there are many, many others, but you want to be sure to get one of good quality and reasonable price. Pre-installation charge should run you less than $15.

Something else to bear in mind when you are purchasing your primary lock is the convenience of removable interchangeable core cylinders, which we recommended earlier for wise superintendents. If you feel that your lock cylinder has been compromised you can change it yourself in a matter of seconds. Instead of removing the whole cylinder you take out only the core, or plug. To do this you require a control key which, when inserted into the keyway, unlocks the core and permits you to remove it with ease. In addition to the control key you will always have on hand a supply of spare cores and keys. On removing the old core, you replace it at once with a new one which responds only to its own key and your control key. In this way you can swiftly render your lock inoperable to anyone in possession of the old key. Then, in your own good time, you can have the old core rekeyed, after which you can return it to your collection of spare cores for use whenever needed. The two leading manufacturers of interchangeable core systems are Best and Falcon—whose cores are actually interchangeable with one another's. Basic price is around $10. Extra cores cost about $6 apiece.

You can get core locks in the form of mortise locks, knob locks, rim locks and padlocks; and you can also get them for interior use on cabinets and drawers. They can be of great value in businesses where employees are responsible for sets of locked drawers and the like. Some banks and airline companies already use them and find them very helpful in reducing security risks. Each employee assigned to a particular section is provided with the appropriate cores and keys. When reassigned, each takes his own cores and keys along with him for use in his new section. This clearly diminishes the possibility of illicit keyholding, and is as much of a protection for the employee as for the company. Other uses in business are practically unlimited—although it must be kept in mind that these cores are not particularly pick-resistant.

But the pick-resistancy of this type of cylinder on your front door is not your main concern. You will be using it in your primary, or convenience, lock; and it is a great convenience.

If you should decide to purchase a removable core cylinder, be sure that the cores are not only removable but *interchangeable*. Plain removable cores are only an imitation of the real thing and are not as good. The system of pinning is inferior, the core itself is not as secure, and the convenience of the system is decidedly limited. Once you take the core out, it won't fit anything else, and you have to rush it right off to the locksmith and have it changed.

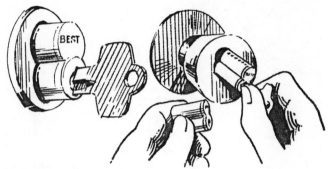

Secondary Locks

These locks are perhaps ill-named, because they are actually primary in your defense system and secondary only in the sense that they are usually installed after the first simple locking mechanism is in place. When installing your good security lock you will have to take into account a number of things about your door and frames: whether they are made of wood, metal or aluminum; whether the door is glass- or otherwise paneled; whether the door is generally sturdy and secure in its frame; whether the quality of the material is good or inferior; whether the stile is wide or narrow; and whether the door swings in or out.

Locks for Wooden Doors and Frames

Many old or middle-aged homes, either apartments or houses, and even some modern dwellings, are equipped with wooden doors and frames. For these, locksmiths—and the police—often recommend the bar-type locks made by Fox and Magic-Eye. These are in wide use on business premises for top protection, and indeed are thought by many people to be more suitable for such premises than for a home. The older ones, particularly, do not particularly thrill the lover of beauty. Yet they are excellent.

Least likely to be used by the homeowner, but nevertheless worth referring to at this stage, is the Fox double bolt or double bar lock. This is designed primarily for wooden doors that swing outward. The bars take the stress off the frame and move it deep into the door jambs. Even if a thief removes the outside hinge pins, the door cannot be moved. Thus the door is protected on both sides. The door is key-operated from the outside for absentee protection, and the outside cylinder is protected by a steel guard plate. For on-the-premises protection you will require an additional lock. Pre-installation cost of the double bar lock is about $60.

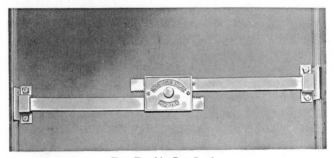

Fox Double Bar Lock

For a wooden door opening inward, one possibility is the Fox brace bar lock. This, you will recall, is the one that literally locks the door up against the floor. The wooden doorframe cannot give, if forced, because there is no weight on it, and the lock cannot be jimmied. The floor bears the brunt of any attack, and the floor, holding the bottom end of the steel brace in its strong metal socket, is not going to stretch or splinter.

This lock is made for locking from the outside only and thus is primarily intended for premises to be guarded in the owner's absence. It does *not* offer protection to anyone within the place; at best it can only lock him in. It must be key operated from without. Some people have bought it without apparently being aware of this until attempting installation, at which point they have tried to install it in such a way as to lock it from the inside as well as from the outside. This incorrect installation defeats their purpose. By the time they finish they succeed only in creating something that offers security from neither inside *nor* outside. They leave the brace vulnerable, so that a thief may be able to manipulate it from outside by pushing a stiff wire under the door or possibly through the interviewer or perhaps even through a hole he cuts in the door itself. If he is lucky, and the householder is not, he may be able to push the bar aside.

If you already have such a lock you can prevent outside

manipulation by asking your locksmith to attach a special safety bracket to the door in such a manner as to protect the socket. He might have to make it especially for you, but he'll know what to do. The bracket acts to deadlock the bar into place and foil all efforts to push it out of locked position.

In normal operation you lock your door from the outside with the key provided, and enter in the same way. When you are inside and it is no longer necessary to keep the brace in position, you can remove it and put it out of sight. Most people prefer to do that, because it is not particularly attractive. In any event, there is no real point in keeping it in place when you are home, for security while inside, you must install an additional lock. Pre-installation cost of the Fox brace lock is about $15.

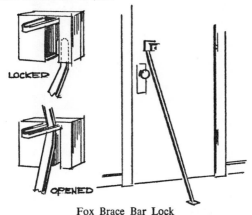

Fox Brace Bar Lock

Magic-Eye has come up with a new bar-type lock that you can lock from both outside and inside. Better yet, they have one model that has a great heavy-duty deadbolt as well as a brace bar. When you go out you lock the bar into place. When you come in, you remove the bar and lock up

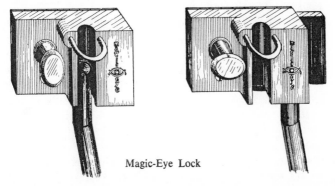

Magic-Eye Lock

with the bolt. This is a superb lock, and Schillizzi recommends it. (He comments, however, that it could be made yet more effective with the use of a pick-resistant or pick-proof cylinder, and recommends the Medeco cylinder because of its pick-proof quality and drill-resistancy.) Over-the-counter cost of the Magic-Eye with the deadbolt is about $22.50.

If all this sounds too complicated for owners of wooden doors, there is a viable alternative. A good, jimmy-proof, vertical deadbolting lock of the Segal variety should do the trick. The Segal itself, as of this writing, can be the most highly recommended. It costs about $15.25, or $17.50 with the nightstop.

Segal Lock

Should you decide to use the Segal lock on a wooden door, it would be wise for you to reinforce the door in the manner described earlier in connection with the bar-type locks. Further, if your budget runs to it, you could install a long angle-iron to protect the stile of the door from top to bottom, and another to reinforce the frame. However, even without this, the Segal lock offers good protection if your door is in good condition and properly installed, and if you replace the cylinder with a pick-resistant cylinder.

Locks for Metal Doors and Frames

The newer houses and apartments are often equipped with metal doors and matching frames. These require a good jimmy-proof deadlock. Here again you can use a lock of the Segal variety, so long as you equip it with a pick-resistant cylinder. Or, by way of a change, you can use the Abloy lock, which is virtually jimmy-proof as well as pick-proof.

It is wisely said by those who know a great deal about these things that there is no such thing as a pick-proof lock. This is probably true; what man can invent he can, no doubt, sooner or later circumvent. But the fact is that there is no record of the Abloy ever having been picked in all the

years of its existence—and the first Abloy locks were made
some fifty years ago. Locksmiths regard it as a real challenge.

There is no question here of substituting cylinders. The
Abloy lock must be used with its own cylinder, and the
Abloy cylinder can only be used with its own lock. Some
times erroneously referred to as a disk tumbler lock, the
Abloy is actually unique in construction. The cylinder principle is based on rotation tumbler or detainer disks that bear
no relationship to the standard springloaded pins, and the
bolt is not a standard bolt at all but a locking bar of unusual
strength and length. Quality of materials and performance
is excellent. Since the lock is of Finnish manufacture it is
not yet available through all locksmiths and there has been
some difficulty in obtaining supplies. But indications are that
demand will force greater distribution.

Like the Segal, the Abloy can be used on both wood and
metal doors, although it can be highly recommended for
metal. Cost of a rim-type dual-cylindered Abloy is around
$21; and of the mortise-type Abloy, about $36.

Abloy Locks

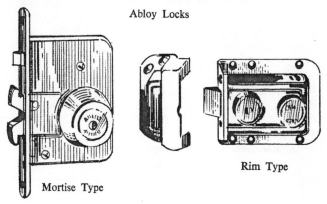

Mortise Type

Rim Type

Locks for Other Doors and Special Conditions

The modern narrow-stile aluminum-and-glass doors pose
special problems. Both doors and frames are usually so narrow and thin that they are extremely flexible, therefore
vulnerable to the jimmy. Furthermore, in such doors, there
is so little space to house the lock that, if a conventional
horizontal bolt were used, it would be so short as to be useless. There simply is no room for a horizontal bolt to retract
in the usual manner. To overcome this problem, owners of
narrow-stile aluminum doors can install one of a variety of
Adams-Rite locks. These can be purchased for swinging

Adams-Rite Lock

doors, sliding doors, single doors and double doors. Depending on the specific use, the lock naturally varies slightly. But the essential principle is that its bolt is pivoted, so that when it is not in use it lies vertically within its housing until it is activated to pivot into the lock strike and lock into a horizontal position. Thus a good, long bolt is ingeniously stored when out of use, to become a sturdy locking bar when pivoted into place. Over-the-counter cost is about $25.

Wood-paneled and glass-paneled doors beg for a double-cylindered Segal lock. The reason for this has already been mentioned: If a thief can succeed in breaking a section of the door and reaching in to turn a locking-unlocking knob, he is in business. You will recall that a double-cylinder lock is a lock that requires a key to get in *and* a key to get out. The most patient of thieves, and the most skillful of thieves, is going to be quite disappointed when he reaches in to find not a thumbturn but a second cylinder.

Swinging glass terrace doors, glass French doors and sliding doors of wood or glass can be protected either by the jimmy-proof, dual-cylinder deadlock or by one of a number of special locking devices such as one of the Adams-Rite locks, Abloy's automatic deadlocking extra strong clawbolt mortise latch, the K-V Plunger lock, the Chicago mortise sliding door lock, or the Loxem Sli-Door Safety Lock. Each of these operates in its own way and serves a particular purpose. Weight, stile, method of opening (swing or slide),

Loxem Sli-Door Lock

and day-to-day usage of the door all have bearing on your choice of lock. Some locks are built to take considerable abuse; others are not, because they don't need to be. The Adams-Rite and the Abloy, for example, incline toward heavy-duty use, while the Loxem (which is very inexpensive) is a lightweight, totally different type of unit often preferred by homeowners. It consists of a cylinder-operated deadbolt which opens by key from the inside only, and comes supplied in a small kit that includes tamper-proof screws. Any homeowner can easily install this unit himself.

The home with the fire escape or other possible window entry should be equipped not only with locks but also a door lock that will force the window-entering thief back to the window to make his exit. Here again the dual-cylindered lock, either the vertical-bolting Segal type or a good mortise lock, serves an excellent purpose. If you use the Segal or other rim-type lock you must mount it with one-way screws, or your thief will be able to take it right off the door.

Abloy makes a certain type of double-sided lock, of fine quality, that serves the same purpose in its own way. It is not, strictly speaking, a double-cylinder lock, but it has a similar effect. In one sense, it is even more practical and convenient than the dual-keyed lock. When you are home at night you lock yourself in with a turnknob, rendering the lock inoperable from without but easy for you to open in a hurry in case of fire or other cause for hasty exit. When you go out and lock the door from outside, the inside knob is automatically frozen into locked position. Thus the thief who taps his way in through the window glass near the fire escape is just as stymied as if he were facing a cylinder.

The brace bar locks, too, lock the window-entering thief inside, or at least drive him back to the window with a minimum of spoils.

Actually, your purpose is not to lock him in. You don't want to confront a probably desperate man when you get home. Therefore, you must not overlook the possibility that circumstances might combine to entrap him, and should weigh this factor carefully in deciding on your lock.

Sal Schillizzi has two stories illustrating the effectiveness of burglar-entrapping locks. Fortunately, they are almost comical from the point of view of the intended victims and speak very highly for the locks; but with a little imagination one can come up with slightly different circumstances that could lead to less happy endings.

One story concerns the ingenious fellow who broke into a

supermarket through the skylight and lowered himself to the floor by rope. He helped himself to whatever he thought he could handle—and then found that all the doors were equipped with double-cylinder locks secured from within as well as without. Well, he tried and he tried, poor fellow, but he couldn't find an exit. The only way out was the skylight through which he had entered. Trouble was, he found it much more difficult to climb up that rope than down it. In fact, he fell and broke his leg. "Guess who called the police?" asks Sal. "*He* did."

Then there's the one about the burglar who came up the fire escape on the backside of the apartment house and encountered a gate on the fire escape window. The window closest to it was about three or four feet away and was blocked with an air conditioner. He took his life in his hands; stretched over, stepped on that air conditioner with his full weight, and raised the window. Safely in (probably unaware that the air conditioner could easily have gone crashing down under him), he rummaged around in the apartment selecting whatever appealed to him. But—little did he know! Someone looking casually out of the rear window of another building had seen him enter the apartment in that daredevil and somewhat unusual way, and had called the police. Pretty soon the thief heard the howl of police sirens; and then he heard a thundering at the door. His immediate reaction was to run to the open window. Too late. Windows were popping open all around him. Anyway, the way out looked harder than it had looked on the way in. He ran to the doors. The front door was equipped with a Fox brace, naturally locked from the outside and totally immovable, and the back door was deadbolted with a double-clyinder jimmy-proof lock. Once more to the front door and the hammering police. They couldn't get in any better than he could get out. It did them no good to demand that he open the door to let them in; he couldn't. In the end he had to go out the way he'd come . . . and, of course, the police were waiting for him at the bottom.

Something equally embarrassing could happen to a thief who is unfortunate enough to meet a particular type of brand-new—but tested—lock unit face to face. This one comes under the category of:

Locks for All Doors That Open Inward

The 3M Electronic Lock Alarm has been especially designed for apartment door protection, but is suitable for all inswinging wood or metal doors. As of this writing, the 3M

Company is still working on a similar device for glass doors, and there is every likelihood that they will soon come up with another fine product.

The present unit is a total door-protection system consisting essentially of a heavy, sawproof deadbolt, outside cylinder, inside thumbturn, chain lock, and battery-powered alarm with microswitch and amplifier. The bolt is extra long and extra strong. The cylinder is of the pin-tumbler type with mushroom drivers. It is a close-tolerance cylinder, made of the highest quality materials, and is therefore pick-resistant—though not pick-proof by any means. However, the alarm takes care of that. As the locksmiths say, "If you can't pick it within four seconds—and nobody's been able to—you've had it, because then the alarm turns on."

A small button located directly beneath the bolt controls the alarm, which can be used for both at-home and absentee protection. Any attempt at break-in by means of caseknifing (which would be futile anyway because of the nature of the deadbolt), jimmying, picking, cylinder pulling, forcing the chain lock while the door is open, or inserting a blank into the keyway with a view to making a duplicate key will activate the pre-entry alarm system within seconds. The alarm produces a loud, pulsating signal which cannot be stifled by a would-be thief; there is no way for him to turn it off, and there are no wires to cut. The correct key, of course, unlocks the door without setting off the alarm. The entire unit features high-strength construction, with all lock-

3M Electronic Lock Alarm

ing parts made of steel or brass.

This device created a surge of nationwide interest when it was first introduced to the public in October 1969, and there is every probability that enthusiasm will increase as more and more people get to know of it. The price is relatively high; high, that is, in comparison with locks that do not have such a multiplicity of protective features. As of this writing, the cost runs in the area of $65 plus $20 for installation. Quote Sal Schillizzi: "It's the greatest thing that's happened in locksmithing in a long time." His words have been echoed by many other locksmiths and at least one well-known ex-con.

Locks for Here and There

There are some locks, or some uses for locks, that don't lend themselves to classification as "primary" or "secondary." So far we have been discussing main entrance doors and what to use on them. But there are other doors that require at least brief consideration.

Exterior Structures

Garage doors, protective store doors, warehouse doors, and doors of storage sheds, barns, cellars and other exterior structures may require padlocks in addition to, or in some cases instead of, other locking devices.

When you get a padlock for your garage or cellar door, get the best you can. Some of them look very impressive but offer little security. Get one that locks on *both* sides. Get one of hardened steel, both case and shackle, and with hardened steel balls that lock in solidly. Get one with a high security pin tumbler cylinder that makes possible a great number of key changes or combinations, so that pickin's aren't so easy. And get one with a good, strong hasp, preferably with a built-in locking bar which, when closed, conceals the screws. If you get one without this bar, install the hasp in such a way that the heads of the heavy-duty screws and bolts are covered by the hinge of the hasp. Finally, get a padlock which is not imprinted with a coded number or symbol. Such a code identifies it so that the least skilled of burglars can read it off and go to the hardware store for a key. If the padlock of your choice does have this code, obliterate it. Some wipe off; others have to be filed off or scratched out of recognition.

Abloy, American and Hurd padlocks can be recommended. Abloy and American offer manipulation-resistant padlocks in which the case and the shackle are both case-hardened. The Hurd padlock differs only in that it does not have a case-hardened case. All three of these padlocks incorporate a feature called positive locking. This means that you cannot snap the shackle into locked position; you must use your key. It also means that you cannot remove your key until you have locked the padlock. This can be a very useful safety feature.

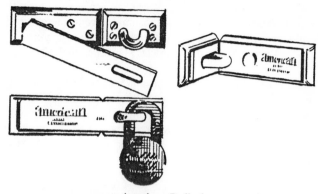

American Padlock

The newer garages seldom require padlocks. We have a choice, these days, between a type of latch lock that is set slightly apart from the handle, a lock-in-the-handle type, and the sophisticated varieties that operate by some system of remote control. Many locksmiths recommend the Taylor latch-type garage door locks and do not particularly care for the lock-in-the-handle type or the "gimmicks."

Interior Doors

The door of the safety room, if any, has already been covered. Here your main consideration is to get in quickly and lock up thoroughly with the least possible delay. Other interior doors, such as the door to the attic or the door at the top of the basement stairs, do not require locks that can be activated hurriedly in time of crisis. Nevertheless, they should have adequate locks that you can activate at night before retiring. Here a good padlock might be just the thing to supplement the simple mechanism that is probably already on the door. Or you might consider substituting, for the original lock, a deadbolt with a good cylinder; or, at the very least, a deadlatch supplemented with a separate barrel bolt. After all, someone with time and patience and a few tools might be able to worm his way in through a cellar or attic window, but that doesn't mean he should be allowed the run of the house as his reward.

Pick-resistant Cylinders

These take us back to your main entrance doors.

One of the finest cylinders you can get is the Abloy. Its major disadvantage is that it is still a little difficult to get; and its second disadvantage, for some people at least, is that the cylinder must be used with its own jimmy-proof lock.

What do you do, then, if you want to replace the cylinder in your existing lock?—in, for example, your jimmy-proof Segal type lock? Among your best bets—in ascending order—are the Illinois Duo, the Miracle Magnetic, and the Medeco.

The Duo cylinder is pick-resistant because it utilizes three sets of tumblers rather than just one set. This makes the pickman's job extremely tricky and time-consuming. The key has fourteen cuts or serratures; one set of five on each edge, and another set of four on one side. The Duo is a fine cylinder, and many locksmiths swear by it.

Duo Cylinder and Key

Slightly higher-priced and even more complex is the Miracle Magnetic. In addition to the standard pin tumblers, this cylinder has a series of magnetic tumblers that correspond with four little magnets within the body of the key. The key magnets activate the magnetic tumblers to release the plug, or core, and permit it to engage or disengage the locking mechanism. Unless the polarity of each magnetic tumbler correctly matches the polarity—and position—of each key magnet, the mechanism will not be activated. This cylinder poses quite a puzzle for the pickman, and presents problems for the fellow with a drill.

Some locksmiths claim that magnetic locks can easily be demagnetized. Others say, "Oh, really? How?" There may be a way, and suggestions have been put forward, but if the purpose is to open up the lock and demagnetization is actually accomplished, then the purpose is simply not achieved. What it boils down to is that, if you do succeed in demagnetizing a magnetic lock (which is difficult at best, in spite of the suggestions), you make that lock even harder to open.

Miracle Magnetic Cylinder and Key

The new Medeco cylinder is not only pick-resistant, but (to date) pick-proof. Its makers think so highly of it that they offer a substantial cash prize to the first person who can pick it. So far, they have kept their money, and indications are that they are not about to lose it. At first glance, both key and cylinder appear to be conventional. But a second glance shows a design of twisting tumblers activated by a key with angular or criss-cross cuts. The correct key, and only the correct key, causes the tumblers to rotate and, in

Medeco Cylinder and Key

turn, unlock the second, or sidebar, locking means.

The Medeco offers a greater variety of key changes than any other lock. In fact, the combinations are virtually unlimited. Of this cylinder, our consultant locksmith says, "I think it's great—the greatest cylinder I've ever seen." It can be used with *any* lock, and it is extremely drill-resistant.

Special machinery and special qualifications are needed to cut the key, which means that only the most highly qualified locksmiths are able to handle this cylinder. It is a high-security product that is suitable for homes, businesses, hotels, and practically any type of premises that you can name.

All the above three cylinders can be purchased and installed for under $30. To be truly effective, they must be installed in a lock body of comparable quality, which raises the price somewhat unless you already have a fine lock on your door.

There are three other cylinders that are often recommended for their pick-resistancy: The Sargent-Keso, The Eagle Three Star, and the Eagle Kno-Pic. They are not actually "kno-pic" or even "no-pick" cylinders, any of them, but they are pick-resistant. However, they all have restricted keys, which may be fine for a government installation or something of similar sort but is not so fine for a private individual.

Restriction of a key means that keys for the locks in question are available from the factory only, and cannot be replaced or duplicated in an emergency by *any* locksmith. The owner's keys are registered in his name with the manufacturer, and if he wants copies he has to submit a written order, with proof of his ownership of the lock and right to the key, to the factory. This can be a great safety measure in that no unauthorized individual can trot off to his local hardware store or locksmith to have an extra key cut, but it can also be a time-wasting nuisance. Many locksmiths, and many private individuals as well, feel that when one needs an extra key in a hurry he needs it in a hurry, and ordering it from the manufacturer is not the speediest way of getting it. A delay of several weeks is not uncommon, although that is not the norm.

The nuisance factor is not the only drawback for the homeowner. Some locksmiths and lock owners feel that it is an invasion of a man's privacy for him to have to register his key under his name and have the details of his purchase recorded on file. Sal Schillizzi's feeling is that for all-round security it is just as well that no record be kept of the ownership of a particular key or keys except by the owner himself. He is not alone in that opinion. However, the quality of these cylinders—and, in fact, the restriction itself—commends itself highly to many people.

So What Else Is New?

The very newest departures ars the keyless locks. These do not employ "cylinders" as we know them. Some of them are based upon electronic principles and some of them are not, but all employ a type of code system rather than a key. Quite a few lock manufacturers are convinced that these locks are the wave of the future.

The advantage of the keyless lock is that it has no key-way, or keyhole. Therefore it is impossible to pick. Marvelous, right? Wrong. Impossible-to-pick is not the same as impossible-to-crack or impossible-to-manipulate. Also, the keyless lock takes a little longer to open, as a rule, than the keyed lock, and most people who are accustomed to using keys are unlikely to adapt easily to any kind of lock that requires a different type of action and somewhat more effort. For these and other reasons, the majority of lock manufacturers and locksmiths incline to the belief that keyed locks, based on some kind of tumbler mechanism, are here to stay.

Combinations and Pushbuttons

Dial combination locks and pushbutton locks differ somewhat in concept and action but offer pretty much the same advantages and disadvantages. In a way they may be more secure than keyed locks because the thief lacks access to their inner parts. But there is more to a lock that its inner coding. To be effective a lock must also be manipulation-proof, and it must activate an effective bolting mechanism. Only the more costly of the combinations fulfill these requirements. Price, generally, runs higher for these locks than for conventional locks—sometimes very much higher.

Perhaps the main disadvantage of the keyless lock is that very fact that it has no key. Both combination and pushbutton locks require that you memorize a sequence of numbers and call upon them whenever you need to get in—coming home from work, staggering home from a party, crawling home after a mugging, running home from a pursuing purse-snatcher. Circumstances that require haste and efficient action are exactly those circumstances that cause the mind to go blank and the fingers to fumble. The faster you want to get in, the greater the chance that you're going to fumble the numbers and further delay yourself. Furthermore, both locks are extremely difficult to operate in the dark. Sure you should have a night light on; but do you? Another disadvantage is that an alert would-be thief can spy out the number sequence of most combinations and pushbuttons and use it himself.

The idea of a combination lock appeals to some people because they figure that what's good enough for a safe is good enough for their front doors. But a front door is not a safe, and the locks are not the same except in their disadvantages. Thieves have been known to spy out safe combinations from a distance; they can spy out doorlock combinations much more easily. It is not uncommon for a would-be thief to pretend to be a polltaker or circular-deliveryman or inspector of some sort, time his arrival to coincide with the homeowner's return, and read off the combination as the homeowner unlocks his door. In fact, a perferctly legitimate delivery boy, salesman, or what you will, may be tempted to do the same thing.

Put yourself in a thief's place: Stare at a key all you like, and it won't tell you any more about getting in than you already know; but watch that combination dial closely, and you have *got* the key. And if you are a thief who is really determined to get into that combination-locked house and can't think of a way to peer over the owner's shoulder without exciting his suspicions, you may go so far as to station yourself in a room or alleyway across the street and read off the combination through a telescope or binoculars or rifleman's scope or whatever best suits your situation. Try being a surveyor, a birdwatcher, a photographer. . . . but enough of these helpful hints to the criminal class.

Good combination locks, these days, have spy-proof dials, that is, they have a protective ring almost all the way around, with only a small section at the top left opening for viewing. This means that if the numbers are to be seen by an unauthorized individual, they have to be spied upon from immediately above. This, undeniably, is awkward.

The pushbutton lock is a little faster to operate than the dial combination, although not very much faster because you have to push the buttons in the correct sequence. Many examples of this variety are completely unprotected from the public view, which again brings up that possibility of someone standing alongside you and watching as you press the buttons. You don't like to tell him not to look and you don't want to shoulder him aside; on the other hand, you don't want to let him see the sequence. It's giving him a key, whether he plans to use it or not.

The simpler versions of this type of lock employ a mechanical bolt mechanism activated by the buttons. Of these, a better-than-basic but still fairly typical example costs about $30 plus installation. The more complex of the pushbutton units are electronic rather than mechanical locks whose buttons are built into a box, which makes sequence-snooping difficult. The cost rock-bottoms at around $200 and climbs from there. Commercial establishments go for this one every once in a while; residences seldom do.

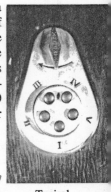

Typical
Pushbutton Lock

Sophisticated . . . or Futuristic . . . Locks

Possibilities are looming that some day some of us may use our own fingerprints to open our own front doors. A recently invented keyless lock employs a photocell and a photographic transparency of a fingerprint; the keyless "key" or combination is the finger that matches the transparency. Shades of James Bond! Could be the day will come when the Enemy transfers the appropriate fingerprint to his Special Lockprint Glove, and triumps once again. But it's a little early to start worrrying about that.

Another interesting innovation is the voiceprint, or voice spectrogram, which is produced by visually "printing" a voice pattern by means of a device called a sound spectrograph. A lock based on the voiceprint would respond only to a specific voice saying a specific phrase; for the voiceprint has a unique ability to distinguish any human voice from any other. Again, one cannot help speculating on the uses to which the Enemy might put his pocket tape recorder. Maybe he could come up with a duplicate "key" and maybe he couldn't. In the meantime, it must be said that such a lock is not yet perfected for public use, and when it does become available it will probably be best suited for a vault or safe requiring a nonmanipulable "combination." (If that ever happens, the lone individual in possession of the special voice and phrase will be in a terribly vulnerable position, but we'll cross *that* bridge when we come to it.)

Locksmiths, when queried as to the possible use of these two sophisticated systems on exterior doors, are somewhat sceptical. These locks, they say, are a little too personalized, for one thing; and for another, "they're too gimmicky."

But—who knows? Maybe some day we will all be using them.

Meanwhile, back in the world of today, there is one more line of door hardware that can give us extra lock protection.

Protective Armoring

The burglar who is faced with a difficult looking lock and a pick-resistant cylinder isn't going to waste much time on finesse. Either he will leave, or he will (if other circumstances favor him) attempt to attack the cylinder or lock housing with all the tools at his disposal. One of his favorite tricks is to forcibly remove the cylinder by wrenching, pulling or pounding. This is not easy for him if he has to work on your good, jimmy-proof, rim-type lock, because with this type of lock the cylinder is *in* the door and thus very difficult to pull out. Furthermore, this sort of lock is equipped with a relocking device which holds even if the cylinder is pulled out, so that you have dual protection.

However, mortise-type locks are not so well protected. They may be excellent in themselves and they may be equipped with the finest of pick-resistant cylinders, but they are more open to attack than the rim locks. The cylinder of the mortise lock protrudes from the outside surface just enough for a forcing tool to get at it. If the cylinder is yanked out of the door it leaves an opening through which the bolt can be manipulated. It is therefore a good idea to protect it with a beveled, case-hardened rim or collar that cannot be wrenched off. Similar rings, though less necessary, are available also for rim locks.

Another way to protect your cylinder is to cover it—all but the core, because you'll still want to insert your key—with a guard plate or shield, of which the most practical is the kind that is set permanently in place and secured with carriage bolts or one-way screws. Another kind is a hinged shield that covers the entire cylinder when it is on guard duty and uncovers it completely when the keyholder wants access to the cylinder. However, this hinged shield must be kept in place with a lock of its own, and while commercial establishments or warehouses may find it useful it is rather a nuisance for a homeowner.

Armored facings and strikes are also available. An armored face plate on the door will do much to protect the lock housing, and an armored strike on the jamb or frame will help to keep the lock engaged even if forcible tampering is attempted. Such armored plates or shields are of particular value on doors opening outward, in which case they are generally angled over the outer edge of the door; but good, sturdy plating on a door that opens inward can be a fine additional deterrent to the most determined of burglars.

One last point on armoring: The locks you choose should, in themselves, be armored. When shopping for door hardware you may be shown two almost identical locks, possibly even of the same brand, whose prices differ quite considerably. Because the two look so similar, and because the mechanism seems to be exactly the same in each, you wonder why you shouldn't settle for the cheaper one. Heft both locks; look closely at the metal; and you will see why the more expensive one is worth your money. It is heavier because it is more solid; it is made of bronze or brass. It will therefore wear well and stand up under heavy traffic and deliberate abuse. The lighter one is *painted* a golden bronze. Underneath that pretty, reassuring color is a zinc alloy—a soft, die-cast metal—which you can literally cut into. This cheaper lock will not only fail to stand up under deliberate abuse but will wear out if subjected to ordinary, everyday traffic. So spend the money.

You might also be shown a lock of pressed steel. This is neither glamorous nor shiny, and it doesn't even look particulary expensive. It happens to be a little on the costly side. You may think that, though it meets your safety requirements, it is no objet d'art for all the money you are asked to spend. However, it does not, like some of the more decorative locks, slice like a hunk of cheese. It wears well, it can take considerable abuse, and it is neat. It is also a good buy.

So think of these things, too, when you are buying door hardware that you hope will give you maximum security. If you shop carefully and steer a middle course between too little lock and too much lock you will be, as the saying goes, safe as houses.

CHAPTER EIGHT

WINDOWS AND WHATNOTS

In case anyone is wondering, a whatnot, for present purposes, can be anything from a window wedge to a file cabinet. Neither of these happens to be an ideal security device.

Windows

It is relatively easy to guard most windows if you take the time and trouble to do it. Available means include gates, bars, wedges, turnlatches and keyed locks. It goes without saying that the windows and frames must be secure and in good condition; the best of locks can do little for a window with a rotten frame or one that can be pried loose. The windows that need your closest attention are those that are on the ground floor, those that open onto fire escapes, those that are *near* fire escapes, those that look out over a ledge, those that are immediately below the roof, and those that are reachable by a climb up a tree or a drainpipe or anything else. In brief, just about all your windows require close attention.

Police officials recommend that all vulnerable windows can be secured, whenever possible, with key-controlled window locks that can lock the window in a closed position as well as in a slightly open position to provide ventilation. Their second choice, suggested primarily for windows that do not lend themselves to keyed locks, is a system of pinning: You drill a hole through two adjoining parts of the window and insert a pin or heavy nail clear through it, thus immobilizing the window with a form of inner wedge. A third choice is the installation of a hinged wedge on the upper sash to prevent the lower window from being raised.

Hardware and dime stores offer all kinds of little gimicks that will wedge your windows shut, and in some cases, hold them partly open to let in nothing more than the night air. Most of them are almost useless for their primary purpose, which is to prevent illegal entry. Let us take a look at just one common example, and then steer ourselves away from these lockless locks.

The standard double-hung window often has a sash lock consisting of a curved turnknob on the top edge of the bottom window and a receptacle on the bottom edge of the top window. This, very likely, is the first thing you will be offered when you go shopping for a window lock—especially if you make the mistake of asking for a "latch." The two latchpieces engage each other more or less effectively when they are new, *if* the windows fit well into their frames, *if* the frames are in good condition, and *if* the two parts of the window meet each other snugly. But these are a lot of "ifs"; and in any event, the "engagement" of two little pieces of metal is easily broken.

Usually the two parts of the window do not fit snugly together, in which case the thief will probably insert a knife between the two sashes and maneuver the latch out of its catch. If the fit seems quite firm and he cannot reach the latch with a knifeblade, he may decide to simply grasp both sides of the lower sash and rotate the window until the latch arm rides out of its catch, permitting the window to be opened without any effort at all.

This "lock," therefore, is the one you do not want. Much, much better is a keyed lock mortised into the window bar, clamping the two portions of the window together until you choose to unclamp them with a key. Such a lock has two main advantages: One, it cannot be seen from outside. Two, the keyed lock (with the key out of the lock and kept away from the reach of an inward-groping arm) will keep the window closed and locked even if the glass is broken.

Effective Locks

So far as Sal Schillizzi is concerned, "You have virtually no window security without a keyed lock. None of the wedge types are particularly good. A window lock, with rare exceptions, must require a key to be effective. Just about any keyless lock, bar one, can be opened from the outside. With a keyed lock the thief must first break the window and then force the lock, which he may or may not be able to do. This gives you another advantage: With a broken window and a forced lock, you can show evidence of forcible entry."

As for that one exceptional keyless lock that is difficult— maybe even impossible—to open from the outside: It is a simple but effective derivation of the standard sash lock that looks superficially similar to the original and is similarly installed on the central, adjoining strips of the sash window. When you rotate the turnlatch to a closed position, it pulls the two parts of the window so tightly together that the most slender of knifeblades cannot be inserted. Further, it has an extra little lever that serves as a snap lock, so that no matter how energetically the window is shaken from the outside the two latchpieces remain firmly linked together. If you look for one of these, ask for the Griptite Sash Lock or its equivalent.

Griptite Sash
Lock

A further refinement on this device is the Loxem Window Sash-Loc. It, too, looks like the standard sash lock, but it locks with a key. Cost is about $3, including tamper-proof screws, and installation is easy.

A somewhat different type, and one that many locksmiths recommend, is a keyed window lock made by Yale. This is screwed into the top edge of the lower window, off to the side so that it is both out of sight and capable of connecting with the side frame of the top window. The tongue of the lock slides through the top of the lower sash into a little metal socket sunk into the side frame of the upper window. A second metal socket is provided with this installation. This is usually sunk into the upper frame about 5 or 6 inches above the first socket, permitting you to raise the lower window or lower the upper window into a fixed open position and breathe a little. The key locks the tongue into place in either position.

Yale Window Lock

Ideal-Security makes its own version of this type of keyed lock. Both are cheap at the price, which is about $3-4.

Fox has an excellent window lock consisting of three parts plus a padlock and key. Because of the padlock you may want to think twice about using it on your fire escape window—although if you keep the key handy at all times you will have no difficulty in getting out when you need to. This lock is also suitable for sliding doors. Cost is about $5.

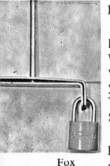

Fox
Window Lock

In spite of your best intentions and efforts to get a keyed lock you may still find yourself being swayed by people who advocate simpler devices for securing your windows. One is that ubiquitous rubber-tipped gadget that holds your window firmly in position and becomes tighter and tighter the more anyone tries to budge it. Then there is the simple wood or metal brace that is used to wedge double-hung windows into place. And there is the turnscrew, with which you can "lock" the window into any position. All of these are quite effective in a limited way. The turnscrew, in particular, is difficult to reach by knife or other device from the outside. But if a small section of the window is broken in the area of the lock, it is easy for a hand to reach in and put these keyless devices out of action in a matter of seconds. The keyed lock presents very much greater difficulties to the burglar. He is obliged to force it, which takes time; or attempt to pick it, which he probably cannot do; or hack out a large enough section of window so that he can crawl through the hole. He is not going to enjoy doing any of these things.

You will probably have noted that the emphasis above has been on wooden windows of the standard sash variety. In fact, wooden windows in good condition are quite easy to secure. The situation in regard to metal- or aluminum-framed windows is somewhat more complex. Most locks are not designed for them.

Some aluminum-framed windows lend themselves to installation of the Fox window lock. Others have to be "pinned," as per the police suggestion. Sometimes it is possible to drill a hole through the existing window catch and insert the pin so as to freeze the catch. Often it is necessary or more effective to drill a hole directly through the adjoining window frames and pin the two together. The pin must fit snugly and should not protrude from either end of the hole—but you must be sure that you can tap it out from the inside with, for example, a nail, or you will be unable to open the window yourself when you need to.

If you do install keyed window locks you will have to make a point of keeping a key available in the area of each window, always in its own place and out of the reach of small children. As a further convenience, you can get all your window locks keyed alike so that one key opens all. You may think that this does away with the need for a key to every window, but it is better to have an excess than to run from one room to another to find a key when you want one.

Gates and Bars

It is unlikely that you will want to protect all your windows with permanent grilles, even if you do like metal ornamentation; but if you are tempted, don't do it. You must leave yourself with ready fire exists. Basement or attic windows can safely be permanently sealed with bars or other grillework. The rest of your windows should preferably be key-locked as described above, and supplemented where appropriate with attractive metalwork. Your fire escape window probably does need a grille—but it should be of a special kind.

Not all states have adequate laws governing the use of gates, bars or grilles at fire escape windows. This means that only too many people throughout the country are guarding these windows more with a view to preventing illegal entry than providing themselves with a ready exit. Many have padlocked grilles; many have bars that are practicaly immovable under panic conditions. The padlocked grille should be all right, but it is so rarely unlocked that the key has a tendency to become mislaid. Immovable bars are deadly. True, the fireman can beat down or wrench off any barrier; but not always in time. You *must not* entrap yourself.

There is now on the market a security grille of expandable construction, designed to be hinge-attached to the inside of the window frame. It is highly burglar-resistant, and yet easy to open from within. Devised by two fireman, this steel gate or grille is approved for use in New York City, and it is to be hoped that it or some equivalent device will soon be accepted nationwide. Hardware store owners and locksmiths in your own state will be able to tell you what your local law permits and the fire department recommends; but even if padlocked grilles are permissible, try to avoid them.

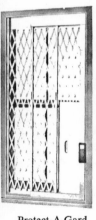

This particular gate is of the folding or accordion type, hinged on one side and latched on the other. The bottom of the gate runs in a track, making it difficult to jimmy. Openings in the grille are too small to permit a burglar to reach through in an attempt to release the latch; and the lock itself, a keyless, latch-type lock, is housed in a steel box to prevent a burglar from attempting to manipulate it with a length of wire. The name of this grill or gate is Protect-A-Gard, and it comes in 11 standard window sizes at a price of about $40. If you cannot find it by name, look for it by type.

Protect-A-Gard
Gate

This type of gate is a fine innovation; an excellent security measure and fireguard combined. If all your efforts fail to turn up something of the sort in your part of the country, raise your voice and ask for it. But whatever you do, don't buy yourself a firetrap.

Inside the House: Safes and Money Chests

A safe is not to keep your money and valuable papers out of the clutch of burglars; a safe is to protect your flammable values from fire. Most home safes (and others as well, for that matter) can be opened easily in a number of ways. If you must keep bills and securities in your home, you should keep them in a money chest. Money chests are designed to be burglary-resistive. They are at their most useful when bolted inside a safe and concealed in (for example) a stereo cabinet, or sunk into concrete in (for example) a closet floor; and when you change the factory combination and *memorize* the new one.

File cabinets are often encountered not only in commercial establishments but in the home. These are excellent receptacles for their purpose, which happens to be privacy. Regrettably, some people seem to think they can be used as safe repositories for money, valuables, or negotiable securities; in other words, as substitutes for money chests. But file cabinets are very easy to open. Most can be jimmied. Most can be unlocked by inserting a long, slender knifeblade alongside a drawer and pressing it against the locking bar within. You can buy an additional locking bar or security bar (Loxem makes them) for the outside of your file cabinet to give it additional security, but don't expect it to make that cabinet as secure as a money chest or even a safe.

There is obviously a great deal more that can be said about money chests and safe-type receptacles, much of which will be freely volunteered by their manufacturers, but here there will be said just one more thing: Only a minimum of cash and valuables should be kept at home. Banks have facilities that homes do not have. Bank your cash, and hire a safe deposit box for private papers and articles that you particularly treasure. A safe deposit box is the safest "safe" by far.

Make Your Door and Window Locks Count

Obviously you cannot keep all your life's possessions in a bank vault. Thieves with opportunity will take anything that can be made to move, even if it means carving up a wall or a floor. If they can't find the money chest, they'll take the coin bank. If they can't find the jewelry, they'll take the paintings . . . or the hi-fi set . . . or the table silver . . . or the antique rocker . . . or the typewriter . . . or the rug . . . or the kitchen appliances . . . or the paneling from the study walls. And if they can't find anything at all that appeals to them, they might just vent their frustration through tearing the place apart. That is why you don't merely want to keep thieves out of your safes and cabinets and drawers and chests and wardrobes and closets; you want to keep them out of the house. Locked receptacles within the home are no substitute for good door and window locks—used consistently and as a matter of habit.

CHAPTER NINE

ALARMS: SCREAMS AND OTHER SIGNALS

It is sometimes said that the noise most likely to deter a thief is a woman's scream. Other people advocate a long, shrill blast on a standard police whistle.

Don't buy this kind of talk. If you're attacked on the street, yes: Man or woman, by all means scream at the top of your lungs . . . if·you can. Or if you are alone in the house and the telephone is out of order and you hear someone getting in through that door or window that you forgot to lock, then you might very well yell out with all your strength—but preferably *after* you have leapt out through some other exit. Better yet, get out quietly and run as quickly as you can to the nearest neighbor, open store, or callbox. A scream is only a last resort. As for the whistle, you might be mistaken for a doorman calling a cab or a kid playing cops and robbers out in the yard. Who listens to a whistle? It may be better than nothing—but not much.

Some observers of the burglary scene are very strong on the idea of dogs. A barking dog is not the burglar's idea of an appropriate welcome, and often proves to be a fine deterrent. Dogs that are big and powerful as well as loud— German Shepherds, for example, and Dobermans—have an additional burglar-scaring quality. However, many law-abiding citizens are not, themselves, capable of handling large, scary dogs. For them, a busy little terrier or yapping Chihuahua may prove to be a better bet. Both terriers and Chihuahuas are alert and extremely vocal. If you like dogs and feel you will enjoy the company of a pet as well as his possibilities as a burglar alarm, you might do very well to invest in this kind of alarm "device."

Remember, though: A dog in the house can sometimes do as much damage as a burglar; a dog has to leave the house on various errands, sometimes to walk with you and sometimes to walk alone, so he can't always be on alarm duty; a dog that is kept out in the yard can be easily silenced by a cruel and cunning thief; and a dog that smiles Hello to everyone in sight and invites them into your home with a friendly wag of the tail may be a joy to have around the house—for the burglar as well as you.

Far better is a mechanical or electronic alarm that guards your home whether you and your dog are there or not.

Indeed, to supplement your locks and provide yourself with maximum security, you will need a good alarm system. Trouble is, a "good" alarm system runs into money. There are very few inexpensive alarms that are at all effective. True, there are a few low-cost unit-per-entry devices that are excellent under certain conditions, but you cannot expect to get real protection from any of the toylike devices that abound in dime and discount stores. Nor can you expect totally nuisance-free use of most of the more costly systems. If you get one that offers all-entry or area protection, you have to be prepared to live with it; you will have to train yourself and your family to use it correctly and not accidentally set off a warning siren by raising a window or treading on the hall rug or sneaking into the kitchen for a midnight snack.

Although there are a great many alarm and sensory devices, there are only three basic categories of alarm systems:

1. Central station alarm systems that bring a direct response from the installing agency (occasionally an alarm company, but more often a protective agency) or the police, or both.

2. Automatic direct dialing systems which, when triggered, telephone a tape-recorded message or series of messages to whomever the user designates.

3. Local, on-the-spot alarms that sound a bell or siren on the premises and which rely on the noise to scare the burglar and alert any interested parties within hearing distance.

Central Station Alarm Systems

The specific workings of these alarm systems, and the sensory or triggering devices which you employ with them, vary somewhat according to the agency with which you are dealing, your own preferences, the locality in which you live, and in some cases on the capacity of the local police force to handle the workload involved.

The Holmes Electric Protective Company offers a prime example of the central station system. Essentially, the tripping of a sensory device in your home or place of business transmits a signal, through leased telephone cable facilities, to the central protective office nearest you, and to the police if you wish. Because the telephone circuits are closed, a thief who attempts to circumvent the alarm system by cutting wires does himself no favor; instead, he automatically creates an alarm condition that registers at once with headquarters.

Each subscriber is served by a module unit in the central station. The incoming alarm signal registers on a galvanometer, which is constantly under the scrutiny of monitoring personnel. Two visual signals and an audible signal alert the operators to the alarm situation and initiate swift response. An electrical reading appears on the galvanometer to apprise the duty-operators of the nature of the intrusion—a door opened, for example, or a window broken. Any trouble on the line that may have caused a false alarm signal is also revealed. Further, Holmes and some other companies maintain their own private power system so that their customers have uninterrupted protection even if there is a public power breakdown.

Homes, stores, banks and all manner of business establishments can thus avail themselves of full-time burglary protection. Daytime holdups can also be dealt with by means of concealed signaling devices strategically located on the premises. These devices can be unobtrusively activated to send a special signal through the agency's central office direct to the police.

Holdup switches, such as footrails and pinch buttons, are available for commercial premises. These are not used in the home, but there are equivalents for the homeowner who feels the need for additional protection. Call buttons, placed wherever they are most likely to come in handy, may be used to summon help whenever an emergency appears to be looming. One such button may be at the bedside, another at the front door, and so on. The additional peace of mind offered by these call buttons is possibly their greatest asset, but they are much more than sugar-coating. Understandably, if the homeowner—particularly a woman alone— becomes aware of the possibility of break-in or other danger, he or she doesn't want to wait for the protection on doors or windows to be activated. With a push of the button, help is on the way even before entry is attempted. This call button can be used even if the alarm is turned off, which makes it admirable for daytime use.

Activation of the standard contact devices or a touch on the call button sends the Help! message flashing along its way to receive a swift response. In the case of Holmes, fully trained armed guards are dispatched to the premises at once, taking with them the client's keys in a sealed envelope and complete instructions relating to the shortest route to his home, the locations of the points of entry, and any information—given to them by the client when making his initial arrangements—that will help them act quickly and appropriately.

A derivative of the call-button system, still being perfected, employs a device that you can carry with you to summon help from outside your home. Basically, it is a remote triggering unit that you can activate when you approach your own premises and, for example, become aware of some suspicious activity on the grounds, or happen to be joined in your apartment house elevator by a threatening stranger. Its signal reaches into your home, activates your alarm system, and brings help in much the same manner as if you had touched an on-the-premises call button.

Some commercial agencies that provide central system alarm services do not have their own private police. They link the installation directly to police headquarters. The system works in much the same way as above, with signals traveling through leased telephone lines to signal-monitoring units at the police central station. These units, each marked with the subscriber's name and address, flash pilot lights, sound alarm horns, indicate line trouble, and pinpoint the source of the summons. Again, help gets on the way with the least possible delay.

The on-the-premises sensors or triggers that may be used in this system—indeed, in any alarm system—cover a range of marvels including photoelectric cells, invisible light, microwave beams, motion detectors, ultrasonics, wall-vibrators, and even radar. You name it—and if you can afford it, you can have it. Depending on the nature of the device, the slightest movement or vibration or minisound can set off your alarm signal. Obviously you must exercise considerable discretion in your choice and use of these detector-triggers. Your place of business may warrant a sophisticated and supersensitive system that can—for example—detect the intake of a breath where there should be no one breathing, but in your home you are almost certainly better off without such complications as invisible light or inaudible sound. It is a great nuisance to all concerned if you house is constantly yelling for all kinds of help that it doesn't need. Most major protective agencies suggest, for the home, a fundamental system of contact devices installed at doors, windows or other openings.

Many, perhaps most, of the central station alarms in current use are "silent" in that they make no sound at the point of origin. These are generally used on commercial premises. Private homes frequently employ a system that produces an audible alarm signal on the premises as well as

127

a signal or signals in the central station. The police generally seem to prefer audible alarms for homes. Their theory is that it is better to frighten the thief away with the noise than wait for help to arrive. The Holmes Company prefers the silent alarm for homes as well as businesses, on the theory that it is better not to tip off the criminal to the fact that he has been detected. They see two advantages here: One, their guards have a much better chance of catching the criminal. Two, the criminal cannot react violently to an alarm that he isn't even aware of, whereas he may do so upon being startled by a noise alarm. Both the police and the protective agencies are in general agreement, however, that when business or residential premises are unoccupied, a silent alarm is best. Nobody on the premises can get hurt—except perhaps the thief.

Protective alarm services of the central station type are provided by such agencies as Holmes, ADT, Wells Fargo, Burns, Pinkerton, and a number of other agencies whose scope of operations is limited to a particular area. Not even the "big name" companies can claim to be completely nationwide as yet. ADT (American District Telegraph) is number one in the trade; it is biggest in terms of accounts and the area it covers. It is also high in excellence. Holmes and Wells Fargo are currently tied in a very big second place; both these organizations are large, widespread, and supremely effective. Burns, primarily an investigative and guard service agency, is a fairly recent entrant into the electronic protective field but is growing rapidly to enhance its already fine reputation. Pinkerton, also essentially an investigative and guard service agency, is an even more recent entrant into the field and tends more to making high-quality alarm devices than central station installations. Your own local telephone directory will help you track down the electric protective agencies in your community. Look under Buglar Alarms in the classified section.

Many security specialists agree that the central system is *the* system for protecting both residential and commercial establishments. But, for homeowners in particular, the cost can be prohibitive. You will have to work out the cost value equation for yourself. Base your figuring on how much you can afford; how much of value you have to protect; how you feel about the safety of your family and yourself; how much you and your family can gain in terms of peace of mind; and what such piece of mind really means to you when it comes to paying cash for it.

Costs of such systems vary from hundreds of dollars to

thousands, depending largely upon the type of sensory system you choose. There is little point in spending top money unless you have a fortune to protect and another fortune to protect it with. According to a Holmes esimate, the installation charge for average home protection should run in the region of $500. On top of this there is a monthly charge that works out to slightly more than a dollar a day, or approximately $30 per month. Charges for the use of the leased telephone wires are included in the monthly rate.

The cost of apartment protection is lower, because there are usually fewer people in individual apartments than there are in houses and because there are fewer accessible points of entry. Installation charges here run to about $200, plus a monthly service charge of around $20. For this you can secure your entrances for absentee as well as on-the-premises protection. Included in the system is a call button, set near the main door, that you can use to summon assistance even when the alarm is off. For instance? Well, you open the door in the daytime to a plausible stranger—and let us hope you use the doorchain—and then you find him trying to force his way in. A touch of the call button, and you know that help is on the way while you do all you can to mash his fingers or his foot.

If you decide that a central station system is for you, choose the agency with care. Ask plenty of questions; shop around. Find out whether the organization is approved by Underwriters Laboratories or insurance companies or both. UL has specific guidelines spelling out the minimum standards that any central station system ought to be able to meet. These standards cover everything from the quality of the equipment to the training and performance of the guards to the time it takes to respond to a call. The major companies more than meet these guidelines. Smaller companies not approved by Underwriters may be perfectly reputable and effective. However, before signing up, you must at least make sure that their facilities meet with *your* approval, that their guards are bonded, and that your insurance company has faith in them.

Automatic Direct Dialing Systems

These sytems, sometimes called "dial-alarms," are based on automatic electronic dialing devices that work through existing telephone systems rather than leased telephone lines. These systems, of which there are a number of variations, are sometimes erroneously classified under "central systems." Presumably this is because they are not local alarms. But they are not exactly central either.

The dial-alarm system is in quite frequent use in businesses and homes. Interference with a contact or other sensory device on the protected premises signals an attachment to your own telephone which then automatically dials one or more numbers. One of the numbers may be that of the protective agency or alarm company that installs the device, another may be the police emergency number if there is one in your city, another may be that of the local precinct or police radio motor patrol, and still another may be your own home or office number—depending on whether the alarm is in your home or in your office. A taped message, repeated several times to each recipient, may or may not bring help rapidly. Results depend very much on the company with which you are dealing. Unfortunately for both the better dial-alarm companies and for the public, there are a number of fringe companies operating in this area that have tended to give the system a bad name. They fall down on equipment, maintenance *and* response; and since these are all essential ingredients, they are obviously supplying you with nothing.

Ballistic Control Corp.'s Telemergency system has an extremely fine track record and is widely used by a number of governmental agencies. Theirs is not by any means the only dial-alarm service that provides quality performance, but this company does offer a fine example of the best that is available in this field. As of this writing they are by far the biggest in their line, and—which is very important to the public—they have managed to achieve a great deal of acceptance among police departments in the areas in which their system is used.

The Ballistics automatic dialing unit is sold on an outright basis to both homes and businesses, and can be connected with any existing telephone system. This means that there is no leasing fee for special telephone lines; when you have bought the system you have paid for it, and need not face a monthly charge.

The Telemergency dial-alarm may be triggered by panic buttons, existing local alarm devices, or remote radio control. When triggered by any of these methods it electronically dials pre-recorded emergency messages to several different telephone numbers. Depending on the needs and wishes of the individual subscriber, the unit can be made to call the local police, the police emergency number, an answering service, and/or what you will. It can even call your doctor or your nearest relative. If a number dialed is busy· or it fails to answer after several rings, the unit automatically calls the next number and the next, repeating the message twice as each number answers. The Ballistics people claim that it is physically impossible for their unit to fault itself, but add that it must be used with good quality sensing equipment. Your existing local alarm might be entirely suitable for tying in with their unit. If it is not, or if you don't have one, Ballistics will install one that offers "maximum protection with minimum equipment." Their recommendation is for fundamental sensing devices rather than super-sophisticated sensory systems.

The dialing unit can summon help silently in case of burglary, holdup or break-in, and can be programmed to handle other types of emergencies (including fire) as well. Any attempt at wire-cutting or tampering with the alarm will activate it at once. Like the central system, it is by no means inexpensive. It may be installed in any type of place from an apartment to a store to a hospital to an art gallery, and of course the price ranges accordingly. But, as a rough guide, let us assume an apartment with three intrudable areas, for example, two doors and a fire escape window, or a front door and two windows, one of which may be a fire escape window. For this you will get three magnetic switches, a shunt lock, and the Telemergency unit. Cost of equipment and installation runs to about $700. As noted above, there is no monthly rental fee to add to the cost; but if the purchaser wishes he may buy the system on a lease-like basis and pay it off monthly over the course of three years.

It is possible to get a similar system for less money. It may very well be an extremely effective one. But in shopping for a dial-alarm it is extremely important to know what you are getting. Some companies do little, if anything, to safeguard their clients against "bugs" or interference on the telephone line, or the probability of frequent false alarms. Others, even if they do provide relatively fault-free installations, supply inadequate response services. Some dial-alarm systems, for example, dial only the number of the installing agency. If this happens to be a protective agency adequately staffed with operators and guards of its own, that's just fine. But if it is a small agency with perhaps only a single monitoring employee on duty at any one time and no guards at all, that's not so fine. What happens then is that the employee calls the police and relays the message. This, clearly, delays action, particularly if it is a busy night for crime and the agency's employee has his work cut out to keep up with the incoming signals—and the police have *their* work cut out to receive calls and respond to them.

Remote Station Alarm Systems

Related to the above non-local systems is another that is usually referred to as the remote station system. It may employ either the central station or the dial-alarm principle on a limited basis. A silent alarm signal is transmitted over telephone lines to be monitored at a remote station. No private protective agency is involved in answering calls; the signal may go to an answering service which will then call the police, or it may go directly to the police department. However, since the remote system is generally used where law enforcement agencies are few and far between, it is not always very effective in terms of speed. In, for instance, a rural area or small town with a small police force, there may be some considerable delay before the police are able to respond. But if that's the best that can be done, then that's the best that you can do. With any luck, it might work out very well.

You will realize, when you shop around, that there are some variations on all the above systems, that quoted prices are only general guidelines, and that agencies mentioned by name are only examples of reputable agencies and by no means the only ones that provide good service. You may very well be able to locate a fine protective agency or alarm company in your own area simply by making inquiries through the police department, your insurance company or your business associates, or by looking in your classified directory. In many cities, telephone companies themselves are in the business of providing telephone alarm systems that you might care to look into. But whatever you do, look carefully.

Largely because of the number of fringe operations in the dial-alarm business, a good many security agents and law enforcement officers feel that the most effective of the above systems is the central station system—specifically one that is installed and monitored by a large, fully-staffed private organization with up-to-date equipment and the capacity to respond swiftly to a large number of calls for help. But it is wrong to assume that you cannot get a good dial-alarm system. You can. Neither system is perfect, and that's about the size of it.

Since both the central station and the dial-alarm systems cost more than a little money, you are going to want to be very sure that you are getting something worthwhile. Whether you are homeowner or businessman, you must accept the possibility that your system may let you down no matter what you spend on it. What looks good at first glance may not be the answer to your particular needs. Glowing claims may not be backed up by the facts. Circumstances beyond anybody's control may provide a loophole for a wily burglar; shoddy work or carelessness may cancel out the value of the finest of equipment. That is why it is so important for you to find out all you can about the system you are contemplating, and why you should, if at all possible, employ one that has *UL* approval or is highly regarded by law enforcement agencies. The alarm or protective company of your choice should have a solid reputation for proper installation of quality equipment, careful maintenance and service, *and* cooperation with local police departments. If your investigation turns up a company that looks good on the surface but reveals itself to have been associated with a great many false alarms, forget it and try something else. False alarms cry wolf, and take up far too much of the police's time.

Some companies (not those mentioned above) tend to concentrate too much on sophisticated gimmicks and too little on the practicalities. Certain sensing devices can be triggered by heavy rain on the roof, a strong gust of wind, a tremor in the earth, or a jet plane flying overhead. Most electric protective agencies will not use such touchy sensors, knowing that if they did they would be keeping themselves mighty busy and their clients highly annoyed. But some of the companies installing the dial-alarms seem to find the expensive gadgetry irresistible. If they combine super-sensing devices with their automatic dialing system, they can create an uncontrollable flood of false alarms in the area undergoing the above-mentioned rain, wind, earth tremor or aircraft traffic. You can imagine the chaos that could very well result, in regard to both the local telephone system and the responding service—namely, in most cases, the police.

Indeed, many installations employing the tape-recorded multiple calls lend themselves to all manner of false alarm situations. A lot of the false signals are due to customer error; many are due to the telephone equipment used; many may be traced to sensitive transistors in the home installation. Too often, the emergency responding services are unable to distinguish between alarms caused by flaws in the equipment, freak "bugs" or acts of nature, customer error, a heavy truck rolling past the premises, or genuine alarm. The better dial-alarm companies do not plague themselves and their customers with these unnecessary evils, because they care for quality and know how to provide it. The others are presumably doing all they can (quite often at the urgent request of the police) to overcome their problems, but in the meantime critical situations involving vast numbers of false alarms have arisen in some of the more heavily populated parts of this country.

The electric protective agencies have been having their problems too. A dismaying note, which applies to even the best of installations, is the growing proficiency of burglars in defeating the central station alarm system and its variations by means of their own extremely sophisticated techniques and electronic equipment. Actually, these people are more than mere burglars; they are thoroughly educated in their chosen field, they are extremely skilled, and they literally make the alarm business their own highly specialized, illegal career. Banks and jewelry stores in major metropolitan areas have, on occasion, been hard hit by these too-ingenious thieves. The agencies providing these systems are currently busily at work to circumvent this circumvention but, while there is no denying *their* ingenuity and diligence, they have their work cut out to keep a step ahead of the Space Age thief.

Enough, however, of dismaying notes. These over-skilled crooks are still a very small minority. The overwhelming majority of thieves do not know how to beat the central alarm systems installed by the major electric protective companies or the automatic electronic dialing systems supplied by the finest of the dial-alarm companies. Many thieves, even the quite highly skilled, are often deterred from making so much as an attempt on an establishment when they realize that it is protected by an agency known to be reputable and effective. A prominent seal on door or window helps

to get across the point that they would do themselves a favor by going elsewhere.

Shopping Hints

Herewith a few final pointers on selecting a central or an automatic dialing alarm system:

Find out exactly how much it is going to cost you and whether you will be getting sufficient value for your money. Ask questions. How much is the installation fee, and what does it include? How high are the monthly charges, if any, and what do they include? Will the company do a thorough security survey of your premises and offer expert, objective —*not* high-pressure—advice on your protection needs, and do it without obligation?

Be aware of the drawbacks of a highly sophisticated sensing system or device, especially if you plan to use it in your home. What devices are offered by the installing agency? What can you get that best meets your needs and your budget?—super-delicate sensory devices to protect the family jewels in your home safe, or top secret papers in your plant vault?—simple yet practical equipment for the doors and windows in your home?—holdup switches for your store?—call buttons?—remote signalling devices?—what else?

Find out exactly what responsive service your money is going to buy you. A watchman at a telephone switchboard? or a fleet of well-trained, armed and disciplined men dispatched instantly in response to signals received on modern monitoring equipment? An answering service only, or four answering numbers to receive your call?

Find out whether or not the alarm system offered is equipped with a standby source of power in event of general power failure. Find out whether or not interference or tampering with your telephone system will put your alarm out of action. Find out if a relay system is included so that your alarm will work even if "bugs" appear. Try to ascertain the company's record of false alarms, and their cause. Find out whether or not the system will be rendered inoperative by the cutting of wires, or if wire-cutting in itself will set off the alarm.

Find out whether or not your alarm is going to reset itself automatically after use. Find out how quickly repairs can be made in case of malfunction or damage: Same day? Twenty-four hours? Forty-eight hours? Reputable firms usually quote twenty-four hours and then do their utmost to cut it down to same-day service.

Find out whether or not your proposed burglar alarm system can be tied in with a fire alarm or other emergency system, either one that you already have or that can be supplied by the company.

And find out just how quickly you can expect assistance to arrive after your alarm has been activated.

Local Alarms

These are the scare-type alarms that are designed to wage psychological warfare against the thief, as well as to alert you, the neighbors, or whoever else happens to be handy, to a break-in attempt. They may employ the same on-the-premises sensory or triggering devices as those used for the central or dial-alarm system, but they are not tied in with a central station or other signal-receiving agency. Local alarms are frequently used in homes or small businesses that cannot meet the cost of the non-local systems. It should be noted that some local alarms cost as much as, or even more than, systems that employ monitoring services.

The police, on the whole, seem to be in favor of noise alarms, particularly if they are highly audible and keep on being highly audible while the thief searches for a way to shut them up. There is nothing that discourages a thief so much—many officers say—as a loudly clanging bell or siren. It should scare off all but the most cool-nerved of burglars. Says the manufacturer of one of the finest local alarm systems available, "You want to chase the burglar. You want to get rid of him. You want to scare him away."

There is another side to the picture, voiced by a private security agent: "If he doesn't scare, you've got problems. If no one hears, you've got problems. If you confront him, you've got problems. And how many times have you heard an alarm siren going on and on and on, with nobody answering it, nobody turning it off, nobody paying any attention? Many times, I'll bet."

He wins his bet.

But the same security agent suggests that there is a way to back up the noisy scare alarm. That way is *light*. A combination of suddenly on-turning lights and audible alarm is suitable for either home or store. What happens is this: When the thief disturbs the sensor or triggering device at door, window or other entryway he sets off not only the noisemaker—preferably a piercing siren—but every light on the premises. Bathed in light and deafened by sound (two things he really despises) the thief who is not a complete nut will depart as rapidly as possible.

A further refinement may best be used on a store, factory or warehouse, although it may be used on a house if the tenant so wishes. The thief makes his attempt on the premises; the bell clangs or the siren blasts off; all the lights go on—and a revolving red light on top of the premises splashes a bright, lurid, flashing glow all around the vicinity. If that doesn't make him leave, he will be found there in pretty short order by interested onlookers and maybe even the police. Normally, however, he won't wait for all the attention he is bound to get if he hangs around.

Also, says the security agent, if you install any alarm in home or store you should use a decal or sticker advertising its presence. Most alarm manufacturers, other than those who specialize in miniature battery-packs that go Boo! in little soft murmurs, provide such stickers. On many of these stickers the wording is such that it is impossible for the burglar to tell whether your alarm is local or tied in with a central system. But even if the phrasing does not give the impression of super-protection, it does help to deter the burglar.

Your choice of local alarm depends, again, on your budget, your preferences, the nature of the premises, and the number of entrances or areas that require guarding.

Shopping for a Local Alarm

Your local hardware stores and locksmiths are bound to stock some kinds of alarm devices. Don't shop with them, though, unless they clearly have a wide range of alarm products or can give you good advice on what, where and how to order. Alarms are specialized products and should, for the most part, be bought through specialized dealerships. This brings us back to the Yellow Pages, or whatever color they happen to be in your city's classified directory. Look up under Burglar Alarms and try to find dealerships offering alarm devices made by Alarm Products, Ademco and Alarmco, Ballistics, Honeywell, Walter Kidde, Pinkerton or Standard. No doubt you will discover distributors and retail outlets in your particular area that offer comparable products. Look into them and see what they offer. Make telephone inquiries, and then go down and see for yourself.

Businessmen are strongly advised to select their alarm systems in close cooperation with their local police and with the help of a manufacturer or distributor of tested alarm products. Many major companies will send—indeed, *prefer* to send—a representative to survey your premises in person and give you expert advice on how to meet your security needs. Homeowners with a little spending money would also be wise to avail themselves of this advice; it comes with all-entry protection, rather than with the (for example) $30 single unit. Single-unit buyers generally have to rely on their own judgment. Homeowners on a low budget will usually find that a well-stocked retail outlet can ordinarily meet their needs, or at least be able to order the required product from the manufacturer. The retailer's charges will consist of retail price plus installation, unless the buyer is a home handyman and can do the job himself. If he is, he can save himself quite a bit of money; installation isn't cheap.

A few thoughts to bear in mind while shopping:

For most practical purposes, fundamental contact devices are to be preferred over sensors based on vibration detection, magnetic fields, radar, infrared rays or ultrasonics. Apart from the fact that the latter systems cost a packet, they are a considerable hindrance to free, legitimate movement. Most of them can easily be tripped accidentally. If they are to be used, they are best used at night in vacant business establishments or in areas around the home that are unlikely to be used after bedtime. Daytime use is limited. Furthermore, some of these would-be sophisticated systems simply do not do an effective job. Those that employ audio-detection, for instance, are either so sensitive that they pick up and react to all manner of extraneous sounds or so dulled by cancellation mikes that they lose all sensitivity.

You must be wary of gimmicky, untested alarm devices that are labeled "pick-proof," particularly those that employ push-buttons mounted outside the door. Of course they can't be picked if they have no keyway, but they can certainly be circumvented in a number of ways. Though alarms of this nature are not prohibitively expensive (they are unit-per-door devices) they do cost more than they are worth, and they are too easily put out of action by a skilled manipulator or a snoop who manages to spy out the sequence.

You should do your best to find a local system that is, as nearly as possible, false-alarm free, thereby minimizing nuisance to yourself, the police, and the neighbors. Similarly, for the benefit of neighbors, police and yourself, you should generally try to avoid any alarm system with a key control switch outside and look for an alarm with an inside switch incorporating a time-delay mechanism that gives you some 12 to 15 seconds to unlock your door, get inside, and turn off your alarm. Outside mounting is thief-tempting; and an inside switch without a time-delay mechanism means that, when the system is turned on, you set off your alarm briefly every time you open your door. It is possible to get a good alarm with an outside switch, but you must make sure that it has a tamper-proof shunt lock that will trip the alarm system if anyone tries to interfere with it.

Always check prices carefully, both for equipment and installation, and be sure you know exactly what you are being offered. Does the price cover the basic sensing unit only, or does it cover the alarm horn? Does it include installation, or are you going to do that job yourself? Prices vary considerably throughout the United States, and even from store to store within a particular community. Installation charges are even more variable. It pays to shop around.

If you decide on an alarm system that relies on house current, try to have a standby power supply or a substitute alarm in case of power failure. If you decide to get a battery-operated alarm, be sure to get long-life batteries and change them every ten to twelve months or whenever your alarm goes off.

And do ask your neighbors ahead of time to call the police on your behalf if your alarm is activated when you are not around . . . or even if you are around. It is just possible that you may not be able to reach the telephone yourself.

You will find very cheap alarms and very expensive ones, but you will find very few effective alarms in the "reasonable" or intermediate price range. The needs of the average person have been somewhat neglected by most alarm manufacturers until recently, so that you will have to search with some care to find anything that fits into a limited budget. Several companies are now in the process of trying to make up for this oversight, and the future holds more promise than the present.

For the man who has everything except a fine alarm system to protect it, Pinkerton offers an excellent alarm device called "Radar-Eye." It is a space alarm, or motion detector, that can be made to cover as many areas inside your house as you wish to cover. With a single antenna you can cover one circle of 50 feet; with an 8-antennae installation you can cover 8 circles of 50 feet . . . which is a lot of coverage. Any thief entering a protected area will set off enough sirens, bells, lights and beacons to send him crashing out of the nearest exit. This installation may be recommended for a commercial establishment or the ground floor of a rather wealthy home. There are several models of this device, but generally speaking the equipment cost will run you—depending on the number of antennae used and areas covered—from a little above $600 to more than $1500, or even higher if the premises are sprawling and the ingresses many. Installation is extra, and is dependent on local labor costs.

It should be stressed that this alarm is not for door and window protection, although the protected areas may be near the entrances; it is space protection that prevents the thief from getting anywhere near your valuables . . . for your blueprints to your heirlooms to the family sleeping upstairs. Actually, this system is at its best when there is no one on the premises.

Incidentally, if any company should offer you, any time within the next few years, a "radar" system for $100 or so—watch it! It isn't going to do you a bit of good. The time will certainly come when radar protective systems are a lot less expensive than they are now, but that time is not the day after tomorrow and a $100 system will necessarily be extremely limited.

Ademco can supply, through its authorized dealers, an "Invisible Ray" employing a photoelectric cell and an invisible light beam. To this basic unit must be added a loud noisemaker, also made by Ademco. The system, with installation charges, runs in the region of $800.

Invisible rays aside, Ademco offers complete premises protection at a cost of from $500 to $800 or more, depending on the nature and size of the home or business establishment. This company prefers to send a representative to your premises for an on-the-job survey to advise you on the best possible system for protecting the place. The "best" is not necessarily the most expensive. According to Ademco, it is the one that fully protects the really vulnerable areas, and the one that meets your esthetic requirements. Essentially, their overall system provides protection for doors, windows, and other entryways, and includes panic buttons or call buttons that can be placed in any part of the establishment. You can, if you wish, use pressure mats as a back-up system. These may be installed at doorways, on stairways or in passages, concealed under runners or rugs or carpeting. When stepped on, they will activate lights, buzzers, sirens, or whatever alarm signal you choose. Ademco's total system is best used in commercial establishment or houses. Their Alarmco affiliate offers apartment security with an alarm system that provides protection for front door, fire escape window, and one "miscellaneous" entrance (for example, a window reachable from ledge or roof) for approximately $200. Alarmco can also supply a fairly low-cost unit-per-entrance alarm device, if that is what best meets your need and your pocket.

Ballistics advocates total system protection and silent signalling via the Telemergency unit, but does offer local devices as well. One such device, quite widely recommended and used, is a door alarm with a magnetic switch. This will go off instantly or with a time delay. It has an outside surface-mounted tamper-proof shunt lock, and a fine reliability record. The price runs in the region of $80, but since the unit can be installed by anybody who knows how to use a screwdriver there need be no question of installation charges. Ballistics also offers pressure mats, or step-on pads, which are about the size of a stair tread and are designed primarily for use on stairs. They can, of course, be used under the welcome mat if you are not in a welcoming mood. Eight ounces of pressure will activate whatever noisemaker to which each mat is wired. Cost per mat, including installation, is about $20. The alarm horn is extra. Soon to be available, if not already on the market by publication date, is another local alarm made by Ballistics. It will be called the Belemergency, and will probably retail at approximately $120 plus installation.

On-Guard makes a one-per-entry device for doors only. It is ideal for apartments, which more often than not have only one doorway to the outer halls. This alarm is a battery operated over the door unit equipped with a time-delay mechanism and a panic button. It retails at about $38, and there need be no installation charge; unless you're absolutely useless as a home handyman you can install it yourself with the six screws provided.

On-Guard also makes window alarms. There are two basic types. One operates on a principle similar to that of the door unit, and can be used on almost any window but particularly on the casement variety. The other, employing a leaf switch, can be recommended especially for the double-hung sash or standard window. Each of these retails at about $5.

Standard Fire Alarm & Signal, Inc., has a basic alarm which they call the Reddi-Eye. It has its own power supply and is easily installed. Under its various guises it may be used to sense smoke, detect temperature changes, monitor electric power, or detect and deter burglars. The burglar alarm is called the Intruder 5. In line with its name, it concentrates mostly on internal traps and uses such detection devices as hidden door switches, pressure-sensitive mats, and panic buttons installed in various locations throughout the home. The power for the alarm horn itself is supplied by a cylinder of Du Pont's Freon aerosol propellant (a liquefied gas). Two or three horns—usually two outside the premises and one inside—are generally used with a typical installation. All are powered by the single cylinder. When the alarm is activated, an extremely loud, pulsating blast from the horns sounds off at once and continues for about five minutes, after which it shuts down and the system resets itself. The cylinder is capable of blowing the horns for fifteen five-minute periods before it needs refilling, and you can check it visually to see when it does. Interested readers will have to check retail prices and installation charges in their own locality, but as a rough guide it can be said that, on an average, an installed assembly costs about $300 to $500. Also available is a do-it-yourself package, which runs you about $250-$300, depending on the number of triggering devices you use.

A small, manual version of Standard's Burglar Alarm is also available. It consists of a Freon-filled signal can with a lever valve and a horn, and although it is hardly small enough to carry around easily in a handbag it is ideal for carrying from room to room, for taking on camping trips, and using on boats. Essentially it is a handwarning device

that can be used as a bedside alarm, particularly by women who are alone at night and fear the possibility of being molested. The unit contains 12 ounces of propellant in a disposable can and sells for about $12. Refills cost $2-3.

Electrically charged foil stripping is available through many alarm companies, the cost depending on the area to be covered. It is ordinarily used on glass door panels and window panes. Stores use it frequently, and some homeowners are beginning to find it quite useful and not unattractive. In fact, it is easily possible to make quite a nice window design out of it or even disguise it altogether. Any breaking or cracking of the glass causes an interruption in the current flow and sets off the alarm. A skilled intruder can defeat this and comparable systems by bridging the circuits; but then, a skilled intruder can eventually learn to defeat just about any alarm system.

Pressure mats, already mentioned, deserve one more reference because they are available through several manufacturers in a variety of styles and sizes. These are nearly always used inside the house, which means that they are activated only *after* the burglar is already in. For this reason, many people like to use such mats in their summer cottages or on their boats for absentee alarm protection, or in their homes when they are out at night. However, even for on-the-premises protection, a wired mat immediately inside the front door, or under the hallway runner, or beneath a vulnerable window, or concealed by a section of wall-to-wall carpeting, or on the first few treads of the stairway, can often prove to be a very useful scare device. Just be sure you stay out of the burglar's way when he tries to get out, that's all.

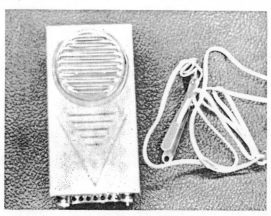

Portable Burglar Alarm

For a small, compact and versatile single-entry alarm, you could do worse than invest in the Apex. It costs less than $5 and is actually a fire *and* burglar alarm with a highly audible siren. Battery-operated, it hooks up easily in a matter of seconds; no screws or tools are required. It is light, small, suitable for doors and windows, and very handy for taking on trips.

The Star Fire and Burglar Alarm offers similar protection at a comparable price. It operates on one flashlight battery and hangs anywhere like a picture. It may be used in homes, offices, automobiles, boats, trailers and hotel rooms with equal ease and suitability.

A little device called Lokalarm, which generally sells for around $3.99, also operates by battery and may be used on any door or window. A sliding bolt or lever that fits into a receiving slot serves as an auxiliary, though keyless, lock. When a door or window is tampered with, and even if its standard lock is defeated, this little gadget helps to keep that door or window closed while at the same time sounding a loud alarm signal.

Dozens of other types of battery alarms are available at prices ranging from about 69¢ to 3 or 4 dollars. Many are made in Hong Kong and employ a little pull-string triggering device. You would do best to regard these with some scepticism; they are not always very reliable, and they serve a very limited function. Some are better than others, and you would be wise to try them out for sound before buying. Sometimes their advertised "loud warning sound" or "ear-splitting noise" wouldn't disturb a fly, much less split a burglar's ear. One good thing about these near-toys is that you can use most of them as portable alarms, for taking with you on trips to set up at your hotel door or window or carry around in your pocket or purse. Protect Alarm, for example, which sells for less than a dollar at Woolworth's, is a cigarette-sized pack that lets off a shriek when a string is pulled or a button is pressed. It cannot, however, be regarded as a substitute for a good home alarm.

A note about wiring: If you are going to have an alarm system that depends on the breaking of an electric circuit, you are going to have wires. These can be unsightly, unless you are lucky enough to employ skilled and careful workmen. To avoid the trouble and mess of nailing down the wires, the 3M Company has come up with self-adhesive wire that can be stuck directly onto walls or floors or other surfaces and easily led under rugs, behind furniture, along the baseboards, or wherever you choose to lay it.

To close out this section on alarms, Sal Schillizzi has a rather sneaky suggestion that will cost you very little money:

"Believe it or not, the cheapest thing you can do—and I would say that, psychologically, it's great—is to start off with a decal outside your door saying that your place is alarm-protected . . . even if you don't have an alarm. Doesn't the burglar suspect it's phony? Maybe. But he doesn't *know*. All you're trying to do, always, is keep a little bit ahead of him. This'll stop the majority of fellows, until they find out it's a hoax. Until this happens, your decal will have served its purpose. You've spent 59¢ or whatever to protect maybe thousands of dollars. As an insurance rate, that's very cheap. Now, if you have your decal, and a good ear-splitting alarm such as those employing horns powered by Freon propellant, you are really going to have something that will give him pause. Remember, if the burglar can't see your alarm, he doesn't know that it's only local. Maybe it's hooked up with a central system. Believe me, he's going to think twice about trying to get into your place. He is going to *run*."

Most, though not all, dime stores carry these decals. They are worth the search, and cheap at the purchase price.

CHAPTER TEN

MORE FOR THE STORE

Small businessmen, particularly neighborhood merchants who run their own stores with small staffs and small funds for buying security, are extremely vulnerable to theft. Actually, the greatest losses in business are due to employee theft and shoplifting, but what's left over is still attractive to the burglar on the prowl. What he cannot know for certain about your home, he *does* know about your business: there is bound to be something of value on the premises. Quite often he knows exactly what it is. If it isn't money it's office equipment and supplies; and if it isn't that, it's clothing, food, liquor, watches, jewelry, leather goods, electrical appliances, tools, machinery parts or other things equally negotiable in the criminal underworld.

Neighborhood merchants' associations are often practical tools for obtaining collective security through the hiring of private patrols or other "watchdog" systems, including alarm-response services, paid for by the contributions of each participating merchant. In some areas, additional police patrols may be requested and provided if the police have sufficient manpower. For an individual merchant able to afford it, it is a good idea to employ a protection agency to plan and set up an overall security system that may or may not include a retainer for follow-up calls or some sort of continued surveillance.

In the main, however, the businessman himself must assume the burden of responsibility for personally protecting his assets against burglary. Like the householder, he must direct his best efforts toward securing all possible points of entry to his establishment. More than the householder, he has to keep in mind the possibility of holdup.

Doors and Frames

First on the agenda of the security-conscious businessman is the question of doors. Security specialists with a mind to great detail sometimes make distinctions between the requirements for front doors, side doors, rear doors and basement doors, but actually the requirements are essentially the same.

Doors and Frames

Solid wooden or metal doors, set into firm frames, are far better protection than wood-paneled or glass-paneled doors. If for budgetary reasons it is not possible for the businessman to exchange his existing flimsy doors for doors of more solid construction, he can reinforce what he has at reasonable cost.

Hollow-cored doors or doors that are constructed of thin wood paneling should be reinforced on the inside with metal sheets, consisting of at least 16 gauge sheet steel, firmly attached with screws. Glass-paneled doors should be covered on the inside with strong iron or steel mesh, or with flat steel bars spaced less than five inches apart. If any doors have outside hinges, they should be provided with nonremovable hinge pins, and the hinges must be secured with nonretractable screws.

Weak frames should be replaced or reinforced. If this is not practicable, but the door is strong or has been reinforced, then a brace or bar type lock should be used so that the security of the lock is not dependent on the door frame.

Door Locks

All doors should be equipped with jimmy-resistant locks and pick-resistant cylinders (see Chapter Seven). If a springlatch is used at all, even as a primary lock, it must be fitted with a deadlocking feature. If for any reason the jimmy-proof Segal type lock or one of the bar-type locks cannot be used on any single door, then that door must be equipped with the best vertical deadbolting mechanism suitable to it.

Doors that are in themselves good barriers by virtue of the fact that they are of solid wood, metal, or *tempered* glass, are relatively simple to secure—bearing in mind that we are always talking about jimmy-resistant locks and pick-resistant cylinders. A single door should be equipped with either a double-cylinder deadlock that is keyed from without and operated from within by a turnknob or handle. The former is always preferable. Double doors should be equipped with this same type of lock on the active leaf, with the inactive leaf to be equipped with flush bolts at top and bottom.

Doors of nontempered glass, or doors that have glass panes adjacent to the frame (that is, close to the lock), require a double-cylinder deadlock. To repeat, this means that they must have a lock that requires a key for opening from within as well as from without. Double glass doors of this sort should be equipped in the same manner as the double doors above.

Overhead doors of the roll-down type should be locked either by electric power or equipped on the inside with slide bolts on the bottom bar and with a pick-resistant cylinder lock. Solid overhead doors, or any other garage style door (accordion, swinging or sliding) should, if not electrically operated, be secured from within with a sturdy crossbar, bolt, or side bar, plus a good cylinder lock. If a door of this type is the only way in and out of the premises, which may be the case in a storage or warehouse setup, then it should be locked from the outside with a jimmy-resistant, pick-resistant lock. If a padlock is used, which may in some cases be advisable, it must have a hardened steel case and shackle and be of highly pick-resistant quality. Coded identification numbers, if any, must be removed before installation.

Private elevator doors that open directly into office, storage or sales areas should be secured with keyed, pick-resistant cylinder locks.

Windows and Other Entryways

All accessible, vulnerable windows must be secured from within or without. Not all "accessible" windows are vulnerable: In some modern buildings the windows are made of material as solid as the buildings themselves, so that they let in nothing but light. These, and their variations, can only be defeated by methods employing explosives, battering rams or similarly forceful devices, and are not really windows as far as the burglar is concerned. He might just as well tunnel his way into the building from an adjoining basement or make a hole in the wall . . . which he has actually been known to do.

For protection purposes, an accessible window is a standard glass or other breakable window that is within 18 feet from the ground, or a ledge, or some other take-off point. The most accessible window of all is one that leads onto a fire escape. Such a window should be equipped with a key-operated inside lock. It must be remembered that persons within must have easy access to the fire escape, therefore it is most necessary to keep window keys near at hand. Depending on local law and the precise nature of the escape window, it may sometimes be preferable to use the inner-latched accordion fire grille described in Chapter Eight.

Other windows, apart from store-front windows, may be key-controlled or secured by bars, mesh or folding gates. Barriers of the latter sort may be installed from the inside or the outside. If they are on the outside, they must be secured with round-headed flush bolts. Should any windows be hinged from the outside, the hinges must be equipped with nonremovable pins.

Display windows are, as many store owners know to their cost, extremely vulnerable. Plate glass is sturdy stuff, but a blow of sufficient force will shatter it. Some merchants still prefer not to obscure their displays with gates or bars of any sort. They are begging for a smash-and-grab job—but they may be able to protect their displays adequately by using special glass. One such material, widely used, admirably resists bricks, hammers and other such objects, but many burglars are finding out that you can hit it with an icepick to make it shatter. The only protective glass approved, as of this writing, by Underwriters' Laboratories is Secur-Lite, made by the Amerada Glass Company. It cracks under repeated blows, and it even bends; but the burglary-resistant glazing material holds it together. A Molotov cocktail, which makes short work of ordinary glass and even most special glass-like materials, actually bounces off this stuff.

Still, most security experts advise the use of metal folding gates to protect store windows and even doors that already have their own security features. These accordion-style gates should, to be effective, be equipped with top and bottom slide tracks and locked with at least one force-resistant, pick-resistant padlock. Again, any coded identification or symbols on the padlock(s) must be obliterated.

Storefronts with a recessed entryway—that is, with a walkway to the door set between two facing display windows—should *not* have gates or bars that are placed flush against the glass to follow the angle of each window. This permits a thief to walk right up to the door in what amounts to a little alleyway that offers him concealment from the sides and from above. Rather, a storefront of this type should be equipped with a folding gate or gates that run clear across it, blocking off the entryway, so that the thief cannot get into an area that offers him any sort of hiding place.

Accessible transoms should preferably be secured with closely spaced metal bars or with a mesh of iron or steel. If such a barrier is on the outside, it must be attached with round-headed flush bolts. Transoms may otherwise be protected, from the inside, with keyed window locks.

Glass skylights should similarly be equipped with closely spaced metal bars or sturdy mesh. Whatever the choice, it should be placed under the skylight and securely fastened.

Hatchways, if not already substantial, should be reinforced on the inside with at least 16 gauge sheet steel firmly attached with screws. Outside hinges must be equipped with nonremovable pins and nonretractable screws. The fastening within should consist of a slide bar, a pair of barrel bolts, a padlock, or a crossbar, depending on local fire laws.

If an air vent is large enough to permit the entry of even the tiniest of thieves, it should be treated as if it were an accessible window.

Sound Barriers

Some form of alarm should always be used as a supplementary security measure. By far the best bet for a store or other business is the silent alarm that summons assistance from a central station. This can be used in the event of either burglary or robbery. Doors, windows, transoms and other points of entry can be completely wired to activate the alarm in case of burglary; alarm buttons or bars hidden in various convenient places around the premises, and activated by a touch of a hand, foot or knee, can summon help silently and surreptitiously in case of holdup. It is even possible to carry a remote switch around in one's pocket. But any central station alarm system, as noted earlier, is a somewhat costly proposition.

A local alarm that rings a bell on the premises is clearly designed to cope with burglary rather than holdup. True, whether you are on the premises or not, the thief will hear the alarm and will presumably be alarmed by it. But in the case of holdup, he may be so alarmed that he will react in panic and perhaps try to shoot his way out before help comes. Thus the best, and safest, use of a local alarm is to frighten the thief while you are *not* there. If you should decide to employ such a device it would be a good idea for you to get on friendly terms with your immediate neighbors, perhaps the tenants upstairs or next door, to make sure that someone notifies the police when your alarm goes off.

For the storekeeper or other businessman who cannot afford a central station alarm system and yet wants to protect himself against holdup, there is an inexpensive but quite practical alternative. This requires the cooperation of another merchant in the immediate neighborhood, preferably next door, and involves the use of a two-way buzzer system. In fact, you might even call it the buddy system. Each merchant has, on the premises or on his person, one or more holdup buttons which he can press in case of emergency. The alarm, silent on the immediate premises, sounds a low-keyed bell or buzzer signal in the neighboring shop. This is the neighbor's cue to take a discreet peek at the scene of action to determine the nature of the emergency, and then quickly call the police. He will also try to note down the license number of any car he sees speeding away from the held-up premises. A number of buddy-merchants have been trying this system very successfully of late. Those who do have such an arrangement for protection during business hours usually install on-the-spot, audible alarms for use when they are absent from the premises.

The police are quite emphatic in recommending, for stores, an alarm with a key-operated, inside shunt switch with a time-delay mechanism. Their feeling is that, if the switch is mounted outside the door where it is accessible to the owner, it is also accessible to the thief. With a little skill he will be able to pick the control lock and deactivate the alarm. This is not the case with all outside switches, but it is usually a good idea to go along with police recommendations. Perhaps your local police officials would be willing to give you their considered opinion of outside shunt locks that are said to be tamper-proof.

Any alarm system you decide upon should be of the type that transmits its alarm signal even if the wire is cut. Thieves are getting good at circumventing basic alarms, and one of their favorite tricks is to cut the wiring. There is no longer any reason why this should help them; in an adequate alarm system the cutting of a wire is either virtually impossible or acts as a trigger in itself. Also, if your alarm system does depend on wiring, it should be equipped with a standby source of power in case of power failure—a not uncommon occurrence in recent years.

Sometimes a decal placed prominently on front door or window, advertising your alarm system without describing it, can be an excellent deterrent in itself. Better not rely on it alone, though; psychology is best backed by something solid. By all means get the best alarm that you can afford. Chances are, it will pretty soon pay for itself.

There is another type of alarm device that the businessman or storeowner might consider, depending on his premises and the type of operation he runs. If he has an emergency exit, specifically a fire door, he is required to keep it open for exit in case of need. However, he naturally doesn't want to leave it unlocked from the outside, nor does he want it to become an emergency escape route for a thief, so he invests in a Detex or a Westware exit control lock-alarm that locks the door from the outside yet permits hasty exit. Cost is under $150.

The way it works is that, to get out, you simply push the panic or paddle bar, and the door opens while an alarm signal simultaneously sounds. The signal may be a loud blast from one or more horns or it may be a buzz from a buzzer if a quieter alarm is desired. The purpose, of course, is to keep track of the traffic going through that door. When the door is opened during business hours, and there is no evident "panic," the alarm calls immediate attention to use of a door that should *not* be used (and must be marked to that effect) except in cases of emergency.

The control lock can also be used for internal security doors, departmental connecting doors, receiving doors, and the like. It can also be used very suitably on doors leading to apartment house roofs, especially in buildings with penthouse apartments or other apartments that are directly accessible from the roof.

If you already have a self-locking lock on a door of this nature, but without the alarm, you can easily add an exit alarm to the upper part of the door. These are also supplied by Detex and Westware.

Detex Exit Control Lock

A fire door equipped in the above manner is legal in most states. To be on the safe side, you had best check your local fire laws before installing any form of panic-bar lock-alarm.

General Security Devices and Practices

It is no more than good business practice to make full use of the best security systems consistent with your budget. If you cannot make all of the suggested security arrangements, you can surely put some of them into effect. Certainly you do not want to tell yourself that, "It can't happen here," or that, "Nothing I do is going to make any difference." Some businessmen are not yet convinced that there is such a thing as a highly pick-resistant cylinder available, and make no attempt to purchase the best they can afford. It is true that there are some highly-touted cylinders on the market that do not live up to their sales pitch, but it is equally true that fine cylinders *are* purchasable by any careful shopper. Other businessmen still cannot see the drawbacks of masterkeying, or dim lighting, or certain kinds of safes, or the practice of handing out spare keys to too many employees and even relatives. They tend to think that changing a system is scarcely worth the trouble. Yet some simple but effective measures can be taken that involve very little expenditure of time, or energy, or cash.

Keys

Good key sense demands that keys be given only to a few responsible members of the staff. Keys that must be kept on the premises should never be left lying around, or hung in an unlocked cabinet, either at night or during the day. It is easy for a temptable employee or unauthorized individual to "borrow" them, just as some employees "borrow" money, and either keep them for later use or have them copied. (The smart employee-thief will copy and return them.)

When a key is lost under doubtful circumstances, or if there is any justifiable suspicion that it has been or could have been copied, the lock cylinder must be changed at once.. For primary locks and interior locks of almost any sort, the interchangeable removable core cylinders made by Best and Falcon can be a great convenience. For the main exterior door lock, the businessman should make use of a highly pick-resistant or pick-proof cylinder, not only because it baffles the pickman but also because it makes key duplication a difficult proposition.

The businessman should avoid a master-keyed lock system whenever he possibly can—and the small businessman nearly always can. If he occupies an office in a master-keyed building, he can either give the management a sealed key for his own lock and make his own cleaning arrangements, or he can go along with the master-key system and make a special effort to secure all receptacles and movable objects on the premises.

Finally, no individual in possession of company or store keys should be permitted to mark them with any sort of identification or keep them on a ring with his house or car keys.

Lighting

A good dose of light scares a thief almost as much as a noise alarm. A bright light illuminating the outside of the premises can be a considerable help, but even better for a store with any amount of window space is all-night interior illumination that spills out through the windows. Best is a combination of interior and exterior lighting. Not only the front entrance but all outside access points—side doors, rear doors, and particularly doors in alleyways—should always be well-lit.

Money chests, or safes with money chests inside them,

should be fully illuminated and placed close to a front window, so that in all their brightness they are fully visible from the street. Cash registers, too, should be under bright light and visible from outside. Why? Certainly not to tempt the thief; rather to make it extremely awkward for him. If he should succeed in getting through one of your carefully secured doors or windows, he will be forced to work on the safe or register under a blaze of light and in full view of whoever may be passing by. He can turn the lights out? Maybe. Hide your switches, protect your wiring, and mount the lighting fixtures as high as you can.

Safes

Safes are for daytime use and for protection of records from fire. Commercial money safes, or money chests, should be used to resist robbery or burglary.

The businessman's best bet for daytime protection of his cash intake is to make frequent bank deposits. In doing so he should make every effort to vary the times and routes of his trip to the bank and to take someone with him whenever he goes . . . preferably not the same person all the time. When it is not possible for him to make frequent bank deposits—and even when it is—he should use the type of money safe that he can keep locked between banking trips and which employs a special locking-unlocking device to help him resist the threats of a holdup man: for example, one that neither he nor his employees can unlock alone. Though the best security containers give way to forcing techniques, particularly thermal burning, the holdup man necessarily tries to do his work quickly and make a quick getaway. Therefore, if he is frustrated by the fact that the employees, and even the employer himself, cannot open the safe for him or give him the combination, he is more than likely to snatch what is loose and make a hasty exit without even attempting the time-consuming task of forcing.

The really frustrating money safe is the drop depository type with the baffled slot cut into the top. This is primarily useful for establishments receiving a constant flow of money throughout the day. All cash that is not required for current use in the register may be dropped into the slot, through which it cannot be removed. Some of these safes are designed to be set into the floor or other appropriate hiding place, so that whoever inserts the money can do it without being seen. Employees are not given keys or combinations and cannot possibly open such a safe on demand. The employer himself has the option of keeping the key off the premises or entrusting the key or combination to a security guard, so that no one working on the premises, including the employer himself, is able to open the safe.

A variety of the baffled-slot safe is the safe with the rotary hopper. Two keys, or a combination known only to a preferably-absentee employer, or both keys and combination, are required to open the door of this safe. If keys are used, only one key is maintained on the premises. Again, employees putting money into the safe are unable to open it even upon the most urgent requests. When the safe must be unlocked, the combination or the second key must be brought in from outside. The thief seldom cares to wait.

When such money safes are used, there should be a prominent sign on the premises, or on the safe itself, to the effect that the safe is of the drop depository type and is not under the control of the people on the premises. This tends to daunt the holdup man. It also helps to make him realize that there isn't much money in the register, and this may just possibly save you an attack on your ready cash.

The above types of money safe are made primarily for protection against daytime holdup. It is best not to rely on money safes for overnight protection of cash or valuables. When this has to be done, the money safe—or the fire-resistant safe with the money chest bolted inside—must be placed in that well-lit, conspicuous location mentioned above, and should be firmly anchored to the floor. Otherwise it should be sunk deep into the floor or wall and thoroughly concealed from searchers.

A variety of the drop depository safe can very well be used by drivers of (for example) bakery or milk trucks and other delivery vans that collect money on delivery, and by salesmen who collect directly for merchandise sold on the spot. This type is called a truck safe, and it can be bolted into the vehicle and either removed bodily or emptied at the receiving station. Again, the driver or salesman can be relieved of all responsibility for key or combination.

These and other types of safes may be purchased from any of the major safe manufacturing companies. Representatives of these firms will be only too glad to discuss the businessman's particular requirements and suggest other security features such as time locks, delayed control locks, removable dials, and silent-signal proximity alarm-locks that transmit a secret signal to the reception area of your choice.

It should go without saying (but it will be said anyway) that the businessman should never leave a written copy of a safe combination anywhere on the premises; that he should make a point of spinning the combination dial several times after each use; and that he should change the combination whenever an employee leaves the firm. These reminders assume a safe with a locking mechanism dependent only on a combination dial. This is not a fault; many combination locks are excellent and virtually nonmanipulable. But it must be borne in mind that if the combination is known among the employees, or if it falls into the wrong hands, the owner of that safe is leaving himself wide open to robbery or burglary. Many businessmen prefer to use a safe with a keyed lock as well as a combination.

Cash Registers

It is wise to keep as little money as possible in the cash register during the day; that is, no more than is actually needed for current transactions. The employer might, for instance, issue instructions to his employees that no more than $50 should be in any register at any one time. Further, he should make it his own responsibility, or the responsibility of a supervisor, to make sure that instructions are followed and the contents of the cash drawers kept down to a reasonable minimum. This is where the drop safe comes in so handy; any excess cash can be slipped into envelopes and dropped immediately into the safe as it accumulates. Thus, a holdup man who cannot get at the safe but can get at the register(s), has to settle for small change.

At night, or at other times when there is no one on the premises, the cash register should be left open, empty, visible from the street if possible, and under illumination. A locked cash register, particularly if not easily visible from the street, is inviting to a thief. Naturally, he hopes there is something in it, so he will either force it or drop it heavily on a rear corner and thus break it open. If at first he doesn't succeed, he'll probably try again. If you have money in the register he will naturally take it. If the register is empty, you needn't have locked it in the first place. Now you wind up with a badly damaged or possibly totally ruined cash register—in itself a very expensive item, possibly worth more than you keep in the drawer.

It is also a good idea to bolt down your registers. Thieves have been known to walk away with them.

In fact, they have been known to walk away with all

kinds of equipment from office typewriters to motel-room TV sets to hospital apparatus. The Bolen safety lock is specifically designed to secure movable equipment. It is what the manufacturers describe as "a bolt within a lock," and features a 7-pin tumber cylinder with a matching, cylindrically shaped key. The Bolen lock fits any standard machine and is easy to apply. With it, you can protect electric typewriters, calculators, dictating machines, cash registers, adding machines, photo copiers, hi-fi components, television sets, electronic devices, and vending machines. (You can even get a special marine model if your business is doing so well that you can afford a boat.) The lock is unobtrusive pick-resistant and wrench-resistant. Cost is $10.95 each, including one key.

Bolen Lock

Checkwriters and Stationery

Your checkwriter and your blank checks should always be kept in a place of safety. In business hours they should be under the care of responsible individuals and out of sight of the casual visitor. In nonbusiness hours, they should be kept under lock and key. Equally important is the care with which you treat all books of sales slips, invoices, order forms, receipts, delivery forms, shipping tickets and anything else that bears the name of your firm. A smart thief can find ways of using these to his own advantage and your loss; therefore you must keep track of them when they are not being used and lock them up when they are not. Even letterheads may be used in a nefarious manner, although this is more in the province of a confidence man than a burglar. Still, whatever you have with your name on—guard it.

Back Rooms and Telephones

Ordinarily your main business phone is near the front or center of your store. This is as it should be. But you may very will be able to make use of an extension or another line in a less frequently used part of the store. For example, in the course of a robbery you might find yourself herded to the back of the store and locked into the storage room, washroom or closet. Or, in the event of holdup attempt, you might have the opportunity to sidle away from the action and lock *yourself* into one of these back rooms. This may not be a very noble thing to do, but it may be a very wise thing *if* you have equipped your washroom and other back rooms with telephone extensions, one of which you can promptly use to summon the police. If you do not have any sort of alarm system, this is the very least you can do to provide yourself with a help-summoning service.

Routine Precautions

Let us assume that you do have a silent alarm system, or that for some reason it is impossible to equip your back rooms with telephone extensions. (It is hard to think of any offhand, but there must be some.) Then you will want to make every effort *not* to be manhandled into a rear room and locked in by a holdup man. The best way to avoid this, nuisance though it may be, is to securely lock all back doors at all times when they are not actually in use and keep the key safely hidden. Do your best to stay in front of the store, near the main door and windows, near the cash register. Let the thief see for himself that the backroom doors are locked and that it will take time to open them. This may not prevent a robbery, but it may save you from being put out of action; and in fact it may be, in itself, a minor delaying maneuver and a factor in throwing the thief off-balance. Also, it helps to keep you, and your encounter with the thief, visible from the street.

Visibility, of course, presupposes that you have not so thoroughly crammed your windows with goods and decorations and signs that no one can see in from the outside anyway. An important precaution is to so arrange your window displays that they attract attention without obstructing the view of the interior of the store. If any part of the store is a little dim at certain times of the day, *light* it. Another important precaution is to try to keep someone with you at all times. A man—and even more, a woman—alone in a store is easily victimized.

Mirrors, freely used and planted on walls, counters, in corners and near ceilings, tend to have a discouraging effect on a would-be thief. So does a closed circuit TV system, either real or prop. These may have little effect on the robber or the burglar, but they will make the cheap snitch or professional booster think twice about shoplifting.

It is only a very unwise businessman who fails to lock all doors to his premises before counting the day's receipts. Otherwise, there he is with his hands full of money, and in through the unlocked door comes. . . !

Finally, the businessman who notices any suspicious circumstance relating possibly to his own place of business or that of his neighbors should immediately notify the police, describe the suspicious circumstance, and then continue to keep his eyes open as things develop. In this way he may just possibly save not only money and goods but even a life.

Much of the above gets us a step or two away from our main subject, that of burglary. But there are so many daylight robberies on small firms and retail stores these days that they cannot be ignored in a discussion that deals with any aspect of theft. Last night's thwarted burglar could be today's robber; today's holdup man might return tonight. And today's juvenile auto thief could be tomorrow's heaven-knows-what. It is one of the unfortunate things about our society that we have to guard ourselves against them all.

CHAPTER ELEVEN

YOUR AUTOMOBILE

"A professional thief or ring of thieves isn't going to be stopped for very long by any kind of alarm or locking system yet devised. Spend as much as you like, and then hide the device as well as you can; he can still get in. He can find it, pick it, deactivate it, get around it, and drive off with it, or he can take that car apart piece by piece."

This was said by a representative of the National Auto Theft Bureau. He was not, however, advocating a policy of passive resistance or total pessimism. He continued: "Don't forget, though, that most cars are stolen after having been left unlocked. Many of them actually have the owners' keys in the ignitions. Well over half of them are stolen by unskilled teenagers who wouldn't even know how to loid open a snaplatch. In fact, an appalling number of them are taken by 15-year-olds—and it's hard to believe that you will find many hardened professionals in this group. And, of course, even professionals prefer an unlocked car.

"Remember, too, that professionals, no matter how skilled they may be, need a certain amount of cover—for example, darkness—and a little time—from a few seconds to a few minutes—to defeat your locks and alarms. Like all thieves, they like things to be made easy for them. More often than not, they will pass up the car with the alarm and extra locking system in favor of the car that does not have this kind of protection."

What it boils down to is that even a little preventive care will foil the majority of would-be thieves. Merely locking the ignition, rolling up the windows, locking all the doors and removing the keys will save *most* cars from theft—not by any means all, but most. These simple measures serve to deter and delay. If a car is locked, the chances of its being stolen are reduced by a good 50 percent. Any added protective features can only have the effect of further thwarting the thief . . . which is precisely what they are supposed to do, and why they should be used. Protection devices can never guarantee security, but the best of them can make car theft too difficult for the amateur and dangerously time-consuming for the pro.

Styles in Stealing

There are essentially four kinds of auto theft: Juvenile

theft, for purposes of joyriding, achieving status, or getting the kind of kick that comes from doing something illegal and dangerous; transportation theft, committed by thieves who need instant getaway transportation from another job or simply a free ride to wherever they feel like going; professional theft of late-model cars, through automobile theft rings or on an individual basis, for purposes of selling to people who are not too fussy about where and how they get their discounts; professional or semi-professional theft of automobiles in order to strip and sell parts.

Joyriders and transportation thieves don't generally care very much what they steal, so long as it has wheels; professionals have somewhat more exacting standards. Only getaway thieves tend to grab at anything that comes to hand. Most auto thieves understandably prefer to operate at night without benefit of witnesses. Nearly two-thirds of all auto thefts occur after dark. Although the thief would love to do his stealing in totally unlit and unobserved areas, he doesn't usually find cars in these ideal locations. Instead he finds them in dim and shadowy places, in "nice" neighborhoods where the residents seem to be oblivious to the possibility of auto theft and wouldn't dream of having nasty bright lights shining outside their windows all night long. He finds them on tree-lined streets, where the branches hang low and the houses are set well back from the sidewalk. He finds them in places that are so busy—such as airport parking lots and shopping center parking areas—that no one notices a little surreptitious activity or can possibly keep track of who owns what car. He finds them lined up at curbs outside apartment houses, far from a streetlamp or from anyone who cares about who takes the cars away as long as they are quiet about it. In fact, he finds them everywhere. The bold and experienced thief, and even the desperate and inexperienced thief, is capable of stealing cars from every conceivable kind of place, including the space under your nose. Over one-half of all cars stolen are taken from the parking places immediately attached to private residences and apartment houses and from streets in residential areas.

When queried as to their preferences, auto thieves cite the following desirable conditions: "Darkness. A late model car parked in a dark street at the top of a hill. Then you can roll it down quietly and start it at the bottom." "A dark street. A door unlocked or a window a little bit open." "A quiet street. A key in the switch. Not many other cars around to box it in." "Who cares about keys? Dim light, thin traffic, that's all you need." "Public parking lot. Key in the ignition. I like it easy." "Unlocked car . . . no alarm . . . open window . . . open parking lot . . . shopping center . . . dark street. . . ." And so on and so on. The expressed preferences vary slightly, but the main message is that veteran thieves infinitely prefer an unlocked car on a dark street or in a thoroughly impersonal parking lot to a locked car on a lighted street with a normal flow of traffic. So do kick-minded teen-agers. Both groups are looking for easy marks. And why not, when there are so many of them around? The car's own basic locks, plus some light and a few potential watchers, can be just that much of a deterrent to the thief that he will move away, knowing that he will be able to find exactly what he wants by strolling an extra block or so.

On the other hand, the really cool professional thief or experienced amateur will usually manage to take the car of his choice even if conditions aren't perfect for him. The pro who is stealing on order for a customer is particularly adept and determined. First he searches diligently for the car that meets his customer's requirements in regard to make, model, year, color and accessories. He may find more than one. If he does, he will certainly choose the one that is going to give him the least trouble; if he has no choice, he will do what he can with what's available. With a little luck, he will be able to drive off in it even if he finds it locked, double-locked, and equipped with an alarm system.

Having located the car of his choice, he will look for an alarm switch, and he will find it whether it is "hidden" or not. (The young amateur may be deterred by the very sight of an alarm switch; not so the pro.) He will look for a spare key magnetically attached to the underside of the fender, and he will use it if it is there. He will look for a mercury switch and be happy to find one, because he can easily take it loose.

If he is a little on the crude side he may smash a quarter pane or force a vent. Ordinarily, though, he neither needs nor wants to damage the car in any way. Armed with one or more of such simple devices as a coathanger, a piece of tinfoil, a screwdriver, a pair of pliers, a paper clip, a beer can opener, a piece of wire with a couple of alligator clips, a knife, and maybe a dime, he can both get in and start the ignition within a very short time. Of course, it does take a little more time than simply getting into an unlocked car and driving away—with a key or a simple substitute—and it also tends to create a certain amount of suspicion if anyone happens to be watching. But on that dimly lighted street, or in that busy parking lot, or near the bottom of that sloping, one-way street behind the apartment house, it can only too easily be done . . . even if the thief has to jerk the lock right out of the door or crawl under the car and cut the battery cable to deactivate the alarm. If, somehow, the locking system foils him and he cannot start the car after getting into it, he may just decide to strip it while it's handy and fill his original order as soon as another likely prospect comes his way.

Amateurs and Pros

Professional theft has taken an alarming upswing in recent years. Increasing numbers of thieves are finding it easy and profitable to beat most auto protection systems in current use, and to make off with parts of complete automobiles which they then dispose of through efficiently organized channels. New York City police, early in 1968, broke up a steal-to-order auto theft ring that had driven off with more than 400 luxury cars within a year. Bargain-hunting customers would put in their orders, specifying make, model, year, color both inside and out, and accessories right down to the exact type of radio and minor details of finish, and the order would be promptly filled. If a car meeting the specifications hadn't already been stolen and stored by the ring, they would go right out and bring one in. For about $3,000 the customer would get $8000 worth of car—really a bargain price, but at the same time an enormous profit for the thieves, considering their minimal capital investment and low overhead.

Professional auto theft has become such big business that some rings actually guarantee to re-steal lemons from their customers. The New York Times of June 4,1969, reported such a case. A late-model luxury car was stolen in Boston and sold to a buyer in Nassau County, New York, for $1200, on the understanding that it was in sound mechanical condition. "The thieves," as the story goes, "guaranteed to steal the car from the buyer if a major defect showed up so that he could realize a sizable profit in his insurance claim. The stolen car had a retail book value of $4,300."

In this case the ring was broken up and presumably at least some of the twenty late-model cars with which the thieves were involved at the time were returned to their original owners, although the news story does not spell out the happy ending. Many such stories do not end happily. By the time stolen cars have been equipped with counterfeit serial plates and their new owners supplied with fake certificates of title, it is difficult indeed to recover them and return them to their rightful owners.

The empty shells of stripped cars are of course useless to their owners even if they are recovered. Thieves engaging in this particular racket are even more difficult to track down than those who sell the cars intact. Ordinarily they do not find it necessary to transport the vehicles for any great distance before they begin their work. Once in a place of safety (a dump, a workshop or a shed, for instance), they strip swiftly and scuttle off to sell the parts and thus divest themselves of the evidence. It takes about 90 minutes for a reasonably skilled operator to pull a car apart. The auto bodies wind up in a dump and the parts with shady auto-parts dealers or carefully selected private buyers.

But even more alarming than this upsurge of professional theft is the fact that the vast majority of auto thefts are still being committed by juveniles with little or no interest in the profit factor—at least in the beginning. Authorities agree that auto theft is primarily a "young man's crime," specifically, a teen-age crime. Why should this be? Probably because young people see hundreds of cars on the roads every day and night of their lives, many of them driven by youngsters scarcely older than themselves, and they itch to get their *own* hands on the steering wheel. A car means power, glamor, excitement and prestige. For young people between the ages of 12 and 16, the taking and driving of a car *just to see what it is like* is one of the strongest and most insistent temptations in life. The temptation is compounded by the opportunities.

The thing is right there, open, ready for the taking. What's wrong with trying it out and showing off a bit? Why not borrow a little status? What's the harm in a little joy-ride? The harm, as many parents know to their sorrow, can reach tragic proportions. Leaving aside, for the moment, the very pertinent question of possible damage or injury, the facts on police files show that auto theft has started more youngsters on a life of crime than has any other criminal act committed in this country. As the National Auto Theft Bureau says, "Police files on hardened criminals usually show auto theft to be the first major offense."

And it *is* a major offense, even for the kid who plans to "just drive it around the block and bring it right back." Maybe he does bring it right back. Perhaps that is the end of it; he may never try it again. Or perhaps, flushed with his success and contemptuous of the authorities for failing to catch him, he does try it again . . . and again . . . and again. And as he drives the "borrowed" car, he is on the road to far more serious offenses.

Adult motorists, particularly those who are parents themselves, must shoulder the responsibility for our nation's number one teen-age crime. At the very least, every car owner should make it a habit to lock up his car as securely as he can. Many first car thefts are impulsive acts that would never occur if the opportunity were not so blatantly presented. An unlocked car, particularly one with the keys in the ignition, is an open invitation to a kid who is looking for something to do . . . or even a kid with no more than normal curiosity about the way things work. Parents who care for their children know how to channel and satisfy this curiosity. They also make clear, before trouble strikes, that auto theft is not a merry lark but a foolish, dangerous act, and a major offense by both moral and legal standards.

The Consequences

This brings us to the question of accidents. Youngsters who steal cars are usually unskilled, inexperienced drivers. Many are not even licensed. Some are actually getting behind the wheel for the first time in their lives. Any single element such as inexperience or nervousness is enough to cause disaster. A combination of inexperience, the desire to show off, and the fear of being caught, can be a deadly one, especially when it escalates into panic. A tragic crash, marked by terrible injury and death, is often the result. The driver himself may escape physically unscathed, but very often other people do not.

Here is a story from the New York Post of September 24, 1969:

> "A 14-year-old boy and two 11-year-old companions were arrested today after allegedly stealing a Sanitation Dept. truck early last night and sending it careening driverless down First Ave., killing one person and injuring five others, three critically. The huge vehicle raced at about 40 mph for two blocks after the boys jumped out, swerving back and forth in the road and finally stopping at 13th St. after leaving devastation and carnage in its wake. Bodies lay everywhere, cars were caved in and a street light was knocked over."

The story continues in all its awful detail, some of which

we can omit. In summary: A woman who was minding a fruit stand was thrown into the air and then run over by the truck, not with the wheels but with the undercarriage. Next the truck hit the light pole, which crashed down upon a woman on the sidewalk. Swerving across the street, it hit a small panel van and sent it slamming into the rear of a parked car. Two boys were crushed between the car and the panel van. A woman leaning against the parked car was severely jolted and injured by the impact. Then the truck, swerving back across the street, hit another car which flew into a woman starting across the street with a bag of groceries in her arms. The woman was crushed up against another car, and groceries splattered all over the street. The last victim, an elderly man, was run over by the truck as he headed home from his janitor's job. As one of the less critically injured parties reported, "I saw this little man get killed. His leg was cut off and his face was crushed. The truck just ran over him. He never had a chance."

The likelihood of accident following auto theft is not confined to youthful thieves. The professional thief is usually an expert driver who takes care to do nothing that will attract attention or damage the vehicle which he intends to sell; and the thief who picks up a car as casually as someone else might thumb a ride is generally a coolheaded individual and an experienced driver. However, both of these types will of necessity increase speed and take chances if chased; and neither of them is immune to panic. As for the thief who has stolen a car to make an emergency getaway, he is usually scared to begin with. And when *he* panics—! Any auto thief, when fleeing the police, will lose at least some of his driving sense and start taking chances that anyone in his right mind wouldn't think of taking. He is running for his liberty, and maybe even his life.

Another hazard may be presented by the condition of the stolen car. Not even automobiles fresh off the assembly line are free from faults. How is the thief to judge the condition and performance of the slightly used car? Or the older, getaway car? It might be dangerously defective. Even supposing it is completely flawless, which is unlikely, it may be a model with which the thief is not totally familiar. His hesitance at the controls introduces a further element of danger.

For whatever reason, or combination of reasons, the fact remains that stolen vehicles often wind up in one sort of wreck or another. Collisions with other vehicles, with utility poles, with buildings, with pedestrians—these are common occurrences. The National Safety Council reports that the crash rate for stolen cars is some 200 times greater than the crash rate for owner-driven vehicles. More than one out of every six vehicles stolen in the U.S. ends up in an accident involving either property or personal damage, and a recent survey in California showed that 24 percent of recovered automobiles had been involved in accidents.

These figures represent not only a shocking loss of life and limb but also a considerable loss in terms of financial damage. Many stolen cars are complete write-offs when they are found—never mind the condition of whatever they have hit. The cost of repairing recovered stolen cars averages out to more than $200 per car. The insurance companies don't like this, especially in view of the great number of cars involved, and that is one good reason why our insurance premiums are high.

There are ways of cutting down considerably on auto theft. Not all of them involve extra spending money.

Basic Theft-Preventive Measures

Here are the inexpensive ways:

1. Avoid parking on dimly-lit streets. Make use of the light of a streetlamp, a well-lit house, a well-lit store. Try to find a parking place where the traffic is fairly heavy, where there are plenty of other cars and pedestrians around.

2. Avoid parking in public lots whose management insists that you leave your ignition key in the car. If you cannot avoid these lots, leave your ignition key *only*. Take your trunk key and all other keys with you.

3. Do not attempt to hide an extra ignition or trunk key under the front fender or anywhere else on or in your car. Thieves know where to look as well as you know how to hide.

4. Do not leave valuables or inviting packages on the seat, dashboard, or any place in view. Lock them in the trunk.

5. Do not leave registration papers, letters, credit cards or anything of any sort of value in the glove compartment or any other compartment inside the car.

6. Roll up and secure all windows.

7. Lock the ignition whenever you can, and lock the doors.

8. Insist on getting a claim check from the parking lot, and ostentatiously note your mileage on it when you leave your car.

9. If your car is delivered to you from a garage, pick it up immediately. Do not let it sit around unattended with a

key in it.

10. Even if leaving your car "just for a second," lock it and take the keys with you.

11. Be careful of your car even when you think it is in a "safe" area; never leave it warming up or otherwise idling outside your house or in your own driveway—unless, of course, you are idling with it.

12. Keep your home garage locked at all times except when you are actually coming or going. Have a bright light in the garage, preferably one that you can control from outside or from within the house. At night, drive in with headlights full on.

To this last point might be added one further suggestion: Inquire through your dealer about a headlight-delay device that keeps your headlights on for a short period after you have parked and locked your car. This can be useful whether you have a garage or not. Some people like to use this device to light up their front doors until they get inside their empty homes at night.

There are many other protective devices now available on the market. Some of the best of them have been incorporated in the current crop of American cars. For this we are largely indebted to various activist consumer groups and individuals—and to the Federal Government.

Federal Anti-Theft Standards

Interestingly enough, the anti-theft measures ordered by the Federal Highway Administration come under the heading of Federal Vehicle Safety Standards, and were promulgated primarily to reduce traffic accidents. Noting the high crash rate for stolen cars, the Director of the National Highway Safety Bureau commented that any vehicle standard that helped to reduce the incidence of auto theft would in itself be a significant contribution to the reduction of highway deaths and injuries. "A reduction in auto thefts," he pointed out, "will contribute a great deal to highway safety, not only by reducing the number of injuries and deaths to those who steal cars, but also in protecting many innocent members of the public who are killed and injured by stolen cars each year."

One of the federal regulations relates to easily visible vehicle identification numbers. This standard requires that all passenger cars manufactured after December 31, 1968, "have an identification number affixed to a permanent structure of the vehicle, located inside the passenger compartment, and readable from the outside of the car without moving any part of the vehicle, by a person standing near the left windshield pillar." The measure is "designed to deter auto thefts by assisting law enforcement agencies in finding stolen cars and apprehending car thieves much faster." The new location of the identification plate is helpful in two ways: First, it permits an investigation officer to read the number without getting into the car. Second, it makes plate substitution difficult; to remove the plate and replace it with a false one involves taking out the whole instrument panel or at least removing the windshield. Any stolen car that can be quickly identified is something of a hot potato for the thief.

The auto industry actually jumped the gun on this one. Nearly all 1968 cars were equipped at time of manufacture with a vehicle identification number located on the instrument panel, close to the windshield and easily readable from outside. All automobiles of more recent make are similarly equipped.

Other automobile standards issued in 1968 became effective on January 1, 1970. According to these standards, all 1970 models must contain three basic improvements designed to combat theft. Every automobile manufacturer is now required to install the following:

1. A device connected to the key-locking system that will remind the driver to remove his key from the ignition after opening the door. One example of such a device is a buzzer that sounds off as soon as the driver's door is opened and goes on buzzing until he removes the ignition key.

2. A transmission and/or steering wheel lock (depending on the type of transmission) which is geared to the key-locking system, so that the removal of the ignition key locks not only the ignition system but also the steering wheel or the transmission or both.

3. Increased lock patterns, or keylock combinations, so that thieves who enter cars with pressure keys or "jiggle" keys are obliged to carry around whole bunches of them where only a few were necessary before. This standard requires each manufacturer to have at least 1,000 different combinations of key-locking systems.

The problem of pressure keys (misnamed "master" keys) used to be one of major proportions. Anyone could buy, at low cost through the mail and absolutely legally, all the keys he needed to fit the autos of his choice. GM began, in the mid 'sixties, to multiply their keylock configurations so that it wasn't all that easy to obtain pressure keys to gain entry to

entire fleets of cars. Since then, all auto makers have
followed suit. Recent legislation quite apart from the lock-
pattern standards issued by the Federal Highway Administration, is making life even more difficult for the pressure-
key thief. Through the cooperation of locksmiths' associations, the sale and possession of pressure keys has been
outlawed altogether in a number of states. Further, Federal
statute now severely limits the indiscriminate advertisement
and sale of these dangerous keys. They are still available,
one way or another, but not nearly so readily as before.

General Motors was ready in '68 with a warning key-in-
the-ignition buzzer. By 1969, a year ahead of time, they had
already installed the required "ignition-plus" anti-theft locking system. The other manufacturers promptly went to work
on their own version of the required lock, and have installed
it in all their new models. Many auto buffs, mechanics and
locksmiths regard GM's version as the best. "Impressive,"
several of them have called it. But whichever manufacturer
has come up with the "best," there is no doubt that all
built-in locks complying with the federal standards are going
to be of considerable help in cutting down on car theft.

In addition to fulfilling the federal requirements, auto
makers have come up with some of their own supplementary
theft-deterrents. Nearly all new cars are equipped with en-
closed or plastic-shielded ignition switch systems to make
them more difficult for the would-be thief to tamper with.
Many cars now have push-down doorlock knobs that are
narrow-shouldered or conical in shape, so that they cannot
be pulled up into unlocked position by a loop of wire slid
down through a slightly open window. A number of autos
are equipped with inside door handles that have to be pulled
inward rather than upward in order to unlatch the door,
again making it difficult for a thief to maneuver the handle
with a wire loop. All in all, the new-car buyer who shops
carefully is in a fairly good position.

The Rest of Us

But what about the motorist who doesn't have a
brand-new car and isn't about to buy one? Maybe he
is happy with his '67 Bobcat or his early '68 Stallion or even
his '64 Bumblebee. Maybe he can't afford to get unstuck
from his present chariot. Or maybe his budget runs only to
used cars. If so, he is going to have to rely on his standard
lock plus his own care, or he is going to have to buy a
protective attachment. He can get everything from an 89¢
phony alarm switch and decal to a $5 stall device to a $35

transmission lock to a $225 super-alarm system. Plus tax in all cases, of course.

There are mercury switches, and there are hood locks (old-fashioned, but coming back into style), and there are wires to link the horn to the domelight switch. There are sirens that go off when the emergency brake is released; there are alarms that will sound off when the car is jacked up; there are ignition keys that jump out of the switch when turned to the "off" position; there are systems that lock the brakes; there are tire lock guards and vibration alarms and all sorts of other things to either help or thoroughly confuse the security-conscious motorist. The friendly neighborhood mechanic (always a good man to consult if he really is friendly—and competent) has usually got his own ideas about hidden switches, cut-offs, by-passes, or what you will, and he is almost bound to have some little packaged gadget to sell you. Either that, or he will be able to recommend some really elaborate system that screams at a touch and is likely to have the whole neighborhood shaking in its boots.

Before investing in anything, give a little thought to what you really want the gadget to do for you and what it actually offers you. Are you going to be able to get used to it? Is it going to be a nuisance? Can it, conceivably, be dangerous?

The Wall Street Journal of August 8, 1968 hypothesizes the following situation:

> "You step into your car, start the engine and pull away from the curb. But you've only gone a few feet when the engine begins to cough. Suddenly, the brakes lock and the sputtering motor dies. A concealed loudspeaker begins bleating, 'Help, help, this car is being stolen,' and your horn starts to blow. As you turn off the ignition in disgust, the key pops out and hits you in the stomach. Next time, you'll remember to turn off the antitheft devices *before* you start the car."

True, you're probably not really likely to be using all those gadgets at one time, but—

> "The nightmare sequence illustrates the potential and the problems in the mass of gadgets being offered to stem the rising tide of auto thefts. . . . Many have been rejected as ingenious but too dangerous for absent-minded car owners."

The National Auto Theft Bureau, though only too happy when people take an interest in extra protection for their cars, says much the same thing in a slightly different way. The Bureau does not recommend any specific products nor does it disparage any, but it does sound a warning note in regard to certain types of devices: "You can get systems that lock the brakes or other effective parts of the car, but you don't want to get anything potentially hazardous; you want to be sure that your anti-theft system is something that can't cause an accident after the car is in motion—either by actually doing what it was supposed to do in order to foil the thief, or by being activated unintentionally. You must *not* be able to accidentally lock the transmission or the brakes while you are driving. You don't want a system that might trap *you* in a nasty situation if you forget to turn off the switch when you get in—such as the brakes locking at the wrong time or the car stalling."

Suppose, now, that you always do remember to use the switch, and that a thief does take your car. A block or a few blocks later it drifts to a stop in the midst of fast-moving traffic, and nothing he can do will get it started again. Now he is the one trapped in a "nasty situation." He will probably have to get out and run, maybe with a cop right after him, and thus you have achieved your purpose. But maybe you haven't, not altogether. Maybe you have foiled a thief and lost a car in the middle of a messy pile-up with other cars and other people. So it's best to think twice about this kind of device.

Not at all dangerous but sometimes very annoying are some types of vibration alarms. The too-sensitive ones are vibrated by any sort of movement, from a strong gust of wind to a child jumping on the car. These alarms are usually wired to the horn, so that when a vibration occurs the horn starts to blow . . . and goes on . . . and on . . . and on. You will need to shop quite cagily if a vibration alarm is what you want, or windy days and fun-loving little children are going to give you a rather annoying time.

Actually, practically any locking device or alarm that you get is going to be something of a nuisance to you. Most of them employ a hidden or at least an extra switch. A lot of people (though you may not be one of them) dislike an extra switch because it gives them more to do, something else to reach for before the car will start. For much the same reason, many people do not like any kind of key ejector system, or device that pops the key out of the ignition in the "off" position. The dislike here is more understandable, because the success of the device depends on the strength of the spring, the weight of the key ring or other key holder, and the number of keys on the ring. What often happens is that a heavily laden key ring will ploop down on the floor and a light key ring will zoom out and hit the driver or pop-fly over into the rear seat. This can be very irritating. The way to avoid it is to use the key case supplied by the manufacturer of the ejector system, and use the case for car keys only.

The best thing to do when buying any lock or alarm is to get the device with which you will feel most safe and comfortable, and which you can easily make a habit of using.

Supplementary Locks

Probably the most effective lock you could get would be one that comes closest to meeting the Federal Standards for built-in antitheft devices. So far, nothing quite comes up to the mark, and it is doubtful whether any supplementary lock will ever be able to; that which is attachable is also detachable, and therefore more vulnerable than a built-in system. Still, there are some worthwhile locks available.

One is a transmission lock called Translok, which is priced in the region of $30-35. It is made for cars with automatic transmission only and is designed for mounting on

Translok

the steering column. Locked by special key, it makes the car virtually immovable. To operate it, the driver puts the gear selector into Park, then pushes the Translok button to lock up the drive line until it is released by key. When the Translok is in operation, thieves cannot move the car even if they succeed in jumping the ignition or starting the engine. This device is available through many auto dealers, locksmiths, auto supply stores and service stations.

Park-lok, available through Lee Myles outlets and some retail stores, operates on the same principle. Designed for automatic tramsmissions only, and specifically for cars with the gear lever on the steering post, it locks the transmission into Park until the driver releases it by key. Again, ignition-jumping will not help the thief. Price is about $35, including installation.

The Deweko Electronic Lock is designed to secure the ignition only, but thoroughly. The basic unit is a removable ignition plug that makes all the electronic connections. When the plug is removed by the owner it is virtually impossible to start the car. Only the owner's very own electronically coded plug, plus his ignition key, will permit the car to start. This coded key lock sells for about $25, or around $35 including installation.

The Securo-Guard Keyless Lock is also designed to protect the ignition, although in a different way. This device is made in Japan and is only just beginning to trickle into this country; you may be able to find one in a well-stocked parts

Securo-Guard Keyless Lock

store. You can use it as well as, or instead of, your standard ignition lock. Instead of a key and a keyway, it employs a two-figure combination on a ten-figure dial. If the correct combination is not selected, the car will not start but the horn will. The retail price is about $20, plus installation by your own mechanic. The manufacturers recommend its use on boats as well as automobiles and motorcycles.

A different kind of device is the Krook-Lok, which locks the steering wheel to the brake pedal. This costs around $15, and there is no installation charge. The driver locks it into place when he leaves the car and removes it when he is ready to drive off. (This is not the kind of brake lock that you can forget to "switch off"; it is a safe and effective device.) The Watch Dog Steering Lock, made in England but available here, does much the same thing at much the same price. It is a self-locking device that is said to fit all cars. The Autolok performs similarly if perhaps not quite so effectively (it is somewhat less sturdy) at a price of about $8. The Car Lok, made by Crowley, is a steering wheel and transmissions lock that performs in accordance with its cost, which is about $5. What the buyer must look for and ask about when considering devices of this nature is the quality of the steel and the effectiveness of any key lock that comes with the system. You really cannot expect a great deal of strength and reliability for less then $10.

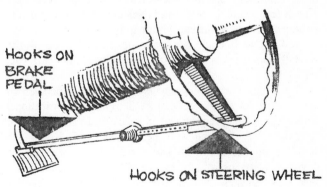

Krook-Lok

The Coach-Gard antitheft device operates on an entirely different principle. It relies on stopping the electricity from reaching the spark plugs, thus creating the effect of a dead battery and preventing the thief from starting the car with pressure keys or jump wires. Installed price is about $13;

do-it-yourself kits may be obtained for $5.

McGard's wheel locks are designed to frustrate the parts-stripper. With these locks, a coded wrench is required to remove the wheels. No other wrench but the owner's will do the job. A package runs to about $20.

On-Guard offers wheel locks at around $8 per set. One of these replaces one lug nut on each wheel. These little locks are key-operated.

The Buss Time-Delay Auto Protector "fools thief—lets him drive away—then stops motor cold." The price is low, under $5, and installation is simple. To activate the device, the owner pulls out a concealed knob on leaving the car. If the car is started without that hidden knob being pushed in, it will run only until the time delay fuse blows and cuts out the car's electrical circuits. This generally takes place within a minute or less.

Steal N' Stall, made by Taroda Industries, operates on a similar principle. The price is the same and installation (in a hidden location) takes about five minutes. The time delay element is destroyed when the car is taken by someone who does not know its secret. The manufacturers say that this fusing out will happen within seconds, "within a block," and that the car cannot be restarted until the element is replaced.

Sparton's Fuel-Lok also provides a stall effect. It consists of an electrically operated valve that cuts off the fuel supply after a few seconds, so that the thief can only keep going for as long as the gas in the carburetor will permit him.

Well . . . we've made our comments on devices of this sort. A stall that stalls a thief can't be *all* bad. But suit yourself!

The Trunk-Gard is especially designed for people who carry valuables in the car trunk. This includes vacationers with their golfing equipment and camera, salesmen with their samples, doctors with their bags, and drivers who simply want protection for their spare tires and tools. The device consists essentially of a very sturdy, case-hardened link chain which, with its strong mounting rackets and hardened padlock, is installed inside the trunk so that it is invisible from the outside. It locked position it permits the trunk to be raised only two or three inches when it is opened with the standard key or if it is forced. A reaching arm can't get very far in that small space, much less take anything out. When the owner wants to open the trunk he first unlocks it in the ordinary way, raises the lid slightly, and

Trunk-Gard

then unlocks the inside padlock with its own special key. The system costs about $9 complete, and can easily be installed in about ten minutes without drilling any holes or doing any damage to their car. Cheaper models of the same device are also available, but of course they are considerably less force-resistant.

Revark sells a hood lock for a little over $3. Kracko has hub cap locks for $2. Replacement door lock knobs are available, usually about $1 a set, under several brand names. They are very smooth of surface and shaped in such a way (tapering to a narrow cone at the top) that they cannot be lifted with a bent wire or coathanger forced in from the outside.

For a full listing of antitheft devices and alarms of all sorts, you might get hold of a catalog put out by Warshawsky & Co., a Chicago auto parts firm. They have an enormous and fascinating selection.

Auto Alarms

The most effective alarms are those that protect all points of entry—that is, doors, trunk and hood—and let out a siren shriek if these entry points are tampered with.

These alarms are controlled by key switch locks which are sometimes "hidden" under a fender or surface-mounted up front or near the trunk. The idea of surface-mounting is to let the amateur see it right away and deter him from making any attempt on the car. The decal helps, too.

The Ademco Vehicle Alarm protects doors, trunk and hood, and has a surface-mounted key switch to control the unit. It is priced at about $28-30, plus installation, and may be obtained with an extra lock for an additional $5. Alarm shoppers should note that installation is a considerable added expense; it just about doubles the cost.

On-Guard offers a similar system, that is, protection for all doors, hood and trunk. The switch is usually fender-mounted. Once the alarm siren is activated, it continues to sound even when the point of entry is closed. The special key must be used to silence and reset the alarm. Price of the unit is $28-30 retail. Installation brings the cost up to perhaps $60 or $65, or possibly less depending on where you get the job done. However, if you have a little skill and some time to spare, and are pretty good at following directions, you can do it for yourself some Saturday afternoon. At least you'll be able to attach the decal.

Babaco Alarm Systems, famous name in vehicle alarms, has a range of units and protective plans to meet particular needs and purposes. Babaco's basic alarm system protects doors, hood and trunk and is powered by the car's battery. The switch, visible and quite formidable looking to a would-be thief, may either be installed up front where it extends right into the engine compartment or near the trunk to extend into the trunk compartment. In many cases (buyer's choice, and 85 percent of buyers choose it) it can be tied right into the electrical circuit so that it protects not only the entry points but the ignition as well.

Not all Babaco alarms are sold outright. One that *is* purchasable as a unit, and the one that is most likely to appeal to the average car owner, is the Defender Alarm. This can be installed by any mechanic, either at a good auto supply store or a service station, and will cost you approximately $75 including installation.

For customers with more specialized needs—for example, salesmen carrying expensive samples, perhaps even drugs—Babaco offers a leased alarm system which includes service and inspection to meet insurance requirements. The initial, first-year charge for the basic system and installation is about $100, with a $50 annual charge thereafter. This charge covers inspection, maintenance, replacements and repairs.

For even more specialized customers Babaco has the Jewelers' Special, a maximum security type of rental and maintenance operation employing Babaco's additional battery system. This is a commercial installation, best used by such people as jewelers and furriers. It can only be supplied by Babaco itself, which has head offices in New York, branches in several major cities, and 250 authorized dealers throughout the country.

The Ramco siren alarm system is sold outright at a cost of about $27. Installation is relatively easy for the slightly skilled, and fairly costly for the unskilled. The unit comes with a heavy duty siren, a key switch lock with two keys, six alarm activator switches, two switch mounting plates, wire for the switches, assorted installation hardware, and two warning decals. Doors, trunk and hood are triggered to sound off when tampered with; only the owner's key can silence the siren.

The Coach-Gard Horn Alarm uses the existing auto horn in alternating blasts, which sound off if doors, hood or trunk are opened. There is a fender-mounted key switch to control the unit, which keeps on activating the horn until it is turned off by key. Basic unit price is $20. To cover professional installation, you're going to have to spend closer to $50.

Sens:tronics offers a do-it-yourself Autolarm, designed to be connected to the horn relay, at a much lower price. It pulsates the car's horn in response to the starting of any electrical circuit; that is, the turning on of the ignition, the turning on of the hood or tail lights, or even opening of the car door so that the dome light goes on, will activate the horn. However, the unit has a delayed activator, so that the legitimate driver has 4 to 6 seconds in which to reach into the car and switch off the alarm system.

Several companies sell units that set off your horn if your car stereo is tampered with. Recotron is one; the cost is a little over $6.

Auto buffs, home handymen or motorists who are lucky enough to enjoy the services of a really competent mechanic, will be able to come up with their own variations of the horn alarm. For the sake of the battery, and the ears of the people in the vicinity, it should be so designed as to pulsate the horn for no more than 2 or 3 minutes before turning itself off; and for the sake of your car's security, it should be able to reset itself repeatedly in case of repeat attempts.

The 89¢ phony alarm mentioned awhile back is called, fairly enough, the False Alarm, and consists of a stick-on switch accompanied by a decal reading, "Protected by the Lectronic Alarm System." So if it scares away one thief, it's worth the 89¢, right?

Mothers! Here is an item of interest from England. It is called the Pram Alarm—perhaps if it gets to our shores it could be renamed the Buggy Buzzer—and it is designed to protect baby in his perambulator. Before leaving her infant outside the store, a London mother of today and perhaps the New York mother of tomorrow plugs in the Pram Alarm, which is set into the body of the carriage and connected to an electronic band around the baby's waist. If anyone attempts to snatch the child, the gadget gives off a loud and prolonged buzz.

It is not always easy to find exactly what you want by way of an auto protection device. Even large auto supply stores, in some areas, carry very little security equipment. You will have to shop around. Furthermore, Pepco Alarm distributors (whoever they may be) may not be active in your area, and you may have to settle for something made by—for example—Zipco. It may be exactly the same thing.

Just be sure that it does satisfy your requirements before you buy it.

To help you keep your car out of the hands of a thief, experts on auto theft offer this advice: Follow the 12 basic theft-preventive measures. Buy lots of insurance. Look in the classified section of the telephone directory in your area and make a note of all the places that sell auto locks and alarms. Then go to them, and get them to demonstrate what they have. Compare prices, compare value to you, compare quality of the items, and check with your own mechanic to see what he has to say about them. If the hidden toggle switch under the dashboard strikes you as being just as useful as a transmission lock, or if the low-priced horn alarm seems effective enough at the price to win you over from the $65 alarm, then go ahead and settle for it. Price isn't everything, and it's your own pocket and your own business after all.

But always remember that your main purpose is to deter and delay the thief. If you achieve this much, you are achieving a lot.

CHAPTER TWELVE

WHEN YOU'RE AWAY FROM HOME

If you plan to be away from home for any length of time on a business or vacation trip you will need to take special precautions to protect what you leave behind as well as what you take with you.

The first order of business is to secure your home to the best of your ability. Try to meet all, or as many as possible, of the items on the following checklist:

Checklist for Absentee Home Protection
1. Make sure that all doors and windows are fully equipped with good security hardware as described in earlier chapters. Check your alarm system to be sure that it is in good operating condition.

2. Make a complete inventory of your prized household possessions, with serial numbers wherever applicable. You should do this anyway, trip or no trip, so that in the event of burglary you will be able to give a complete, accurate and detailed list of stolen property to your insurance company as well as to the police. Note and describe all prized household goods, including fine pieces of furniture, TV sets, radios,

phonographs, clocks, typewriters, furs, jewelry, silver, paintings and other art works, fine linens, electrical applicances, and all photographic equipment. Copy down all registration and serial numbers, and have photographs taken of your jewelry. Insurance companies quite rightly demand all the information they can get, and the police need it to track down stolen property. (Police officers have often been heard to say that they have storehouses full of recovered property, but are unable to return it to their rightful owners because they have no way of identifying it.)

3. Having made your list, take the extra precaution of storing your best furs with a reliable company, banking excess cash, and putting jewelry in a bank safe deposit box.

4. Notify your local police of your intended absence. In most communities it is possible to make arrangements with the police for an occasional or even regular checkup on your home. Or notify your home protection service, if you use one.

5. Notify a trusted neighbor, or a couple of trusted neighbors, that you are going to be away. Neighbors can be of help in any of several ways: They can keep an eye on your house and notify the police if they see anything suspicious; they can be kept informed of your whereabouts so that you can be reached in case of emergency; they can be given a key and written authority to enter your house whenever it may seem necessary or helpful; they can help disguise or remove the signs of your absence by picking up circulars and samples that would otherwise accumulate; and they can even take care of unkempt grass and mail-collection if for some reason you cannot make, or do not want to make, other arrangements. Naturally, you should offer reciprocal services when your turn comes.

6. If you live in a house with any grounds to speak of, and if you are going to be away for any appreciable length of time, make definite arrangements to have the grounds kept reasonably clean. If those helpful neighbors can't do it, somebody else should. Every once in a while the leaves must be raked, the grass cut, maybe even the hedge trimmed, depending on the seasonal requirements.

7. Cancel all deliveries that you are accustomed to receiving regularly—milk, eggs, newspapers, the Friday fish, and so on. Make such cancellations in person, by mail, or by phone; do *not* leave notes for delivery men.

8. Notify your post office that you will be away for a

specified length of time and ask them to hold your mail for you. Or ask a friend to check your mailbox daily.

9. If you live in an apartment, be sure to tell the landlord or superintendent of your intended absence, and let him know where and how you can be reached in an emergency.

10. Avoid notifying the local newspaper, or too many of your neighbors and local merchants, of your forthcoming trip. An official announcement may be a direct invitation to theft, and even casual talk may spread too far. You want just enough people to know about your trip; *only* just enough, and not too many.

11. Under no circumstances should you leave a key in a "hidden" place. Nor should you leave a note, no matter how cleverly devised, telling where a key may be found.

12. Invest in one or two automatic light timers that will turn a couple of your inside lights on and off at pre-set hours. The lights should be in separate rooms and the timer or timers set so that the lights go on and off at different times, giving the illusion that someone is home and moving about the house. You can also, if you wish, use a timer to turn a radio on and off at certain times. For your outside light you may prefer to use the photoelectric device that turns the light on at night and off in the daytime. All of these devices are simple and reasonably priced (about $6-8). For your inside timer, be sure you get the repeater kind that resets itself automatically, otherwise it is only good for one use.

13. Attend to your telephone. Preferably, do not disconnect it for the period of your absence. Any would-be thief, trying one of those "Is Harry home?" calls will be immediately alerted that Harry is not about to be home for some considerable time, nor is anyone else. It is better to leave the phone connected but muffled, so that extended, unanswered ringing is not heard from outside the house as well as over the line. It is even better to make temporary use of an answering service. (If you ever employ an answering service, you should give strict instructions that your address should never be given out to anyone over the phone.)

14. Leave your window shades halfway up or your venetian blinds partly open, and don't draw the curtains all the way across. If you blank out your windows altogether, or leave them too exposed, you will give away the fact that your house is unoccupied. What you want to do is, in every way possible, to give the impression that life goes on as

usual at your home.

15. *Use* your locks and security devices—all of them. Double-check all entry points, and lock up the ladder in the garage.

Basic Preparations for Your Trip

Wherever you are going and whatever you are going to do, you will need some form of negotiable tender—namely, money. Keep cash down to a minimum. Buy travelers' checks. And if you carry credit cards, as most people do these days, keep them separate from your wallet and in the safest of your inside pockets. Before you leave, be sure you know the notification procedures and the address of the issuing company in the event of loss or theft.

Label your luggage carefully. In addition to tags on the outside, tape a card to the inside of each lid. Don't be tempted to buy expensive, beautiful luggage with superior-looking locks; the locks may be fine, but the luggage can easily be carried away intact. Rather buy cheaper luggage. There's less chance of it being stolen.

Try to make your departure as inconspicuous as possible. If you are being called for by cab to take you to the airport or the pier, it is none too easy to leave unobtrusively. A discreet apartment house doorman can be a big help, but in front of your own house you just have to load up as quickly as possible and be on your way.

If you are traveling in your own car, you are a little better off. You can choose your own loading time and, up to a point, place. An alleyway is better than the street. A driveway is better than an alleyway. And a garage is better than anything. If you can take your luggage out of the back door and load it directly into your garaged car, you are really in luck.

Have your car thoroughly serviced before you leave to minimize the possibility of breakdown on the road. Check its auxiliary lock(s) and alarm. Be sure to get a Trunk-Gard if there is any likelihood that you are going to have to park it in the open or in a public lot anywhere along your trip. At the very least, make it a practice to *lock it and pocket the key* whenever you have to leave your car.

Equip yourself with a couple of travel locks, to be described in detail in the section headed *Hotels and Motels*.

Safe Driving Practices

How carefully and how well you ought to drive is not

going to be discussed here. You may yourself have to discuss it with a traffic officer, but that's another matter. What is relevant now is what you do to protect yourself against auto thieves and other kinds of people who prey on cars and drivers. Herewith, a few tips to foil the predators:

1. Keep all your doors locked, particularly when driving alone.

2. Keep your windows rolled up as high as is consistent with your ventilation needs. Do this especially when you are driving alone, especially at night, and especially when you have to stop frequently for traffic lights or stop signs.

3. Try, when driving at night, to keep on well-lighted, well-traveled roads and streets. Avoid the shortcut through the woods or the backyards of the city.

4. If you have a convertible, keep the top up when you are driving alone at night or when you are driving—with or without company—through unfamiliar areas or possible trouble spots.

5. *Never pick up a stranger.* Whether you are a man or a woman, whether the stranger is a man or a woman, whether you are alone or have company, whether the stranger is well-dressed, shabbily dressed or uniformed, *never pick up a stranger.*

6. Don't let anyone but a police officer flag you down. If you see an apparently genuine accident, stop with your car well out of the way, find out what you can do to help (such as rush the fastest possible message to the police), and then get on with it. Be sure you know your state laws regarding what to do and when to stay at the scene of an accident. If someone flags you down and you cannot immediately see what the trouble is, slow down without stopping and look the situation over; or stop with doors locked and windows rolled nearly all the way up, and inquire what the problem is. In either event you should report the flagdown as soon as you reach a telephone.

7. If you should ever find yourself fooled into picking up someone who turns out to be an undesirable companion, drive as fast as you can so that any attack on you is impossible. Make yourself conspicuous; lean on the horn, and break the speed limit just for once. Stop only when a police car flags you down for speeding or when you get to a well-lit place with lots of people around, preferably a police station, firehouse or service station. Similarly, if someone tries to get into your car while you are stopped at a light, and if you have any maneuvering room, accelerate at once

and lean on the horn. It is better to jump a red light—if the intersection is clear—than let someone break into your car. If the intersection is not clear, make whatever maneuver you can and all the noise you're capable of.

8. If you have car trouble on the road, do the best you can to force Old Betsy to stagger on until you reach some sign of civilization. If she can't manage this, coast her onto the shoulder and check that all your doors and windows are secured, except for the door you are going to use immediately, and then let yourself out of the car for just long enough to put your SOS measures into effect. Raise the trunk lid and the hood. Tie a cloth, preferably a white handkerchief, to the top of your radio antenna or to the front door handle on the traffic side. Hop back into the car, turn on whatever emergency flashing equipment you may have, and lock yourself in. Even the driver's seat window need only be open a couple of inches. When help comes, be sure that it's genuine. Unless you are carrying a carload of tough friends, *do not* roll down the window or open the door to explain your predicament to any helpful looking stranger . . . especially if he is also carrying a carload of tough friends. You can tell him what the problem is and be as grateful as you like through the partly open window. Tell him all you want is that he should send help back to you.

This is particularly important for a woman or a couple of women driving alone. It's tough to have to be so suspicious, but that's the way it goes. If a nice man pulls over and offers to take the woman driver to the nearest gas or police station, she should thank him warmly and decline his offer. It would be much nicer, she should indicate, as well as simpler all round, if he were to go on his way with all possible haste and look for a cop or a phone. If the gentlemen persists in being too helpful and tries to force his way into the car, the lady should lean on the horn. If she has a portable alarm at hand, or any other alarm siren that she can activate, she might as well put that to work as well.

9. When you park your car for the night, try to leave it in a well-lit area. If you can leave it in an attended hotel garage or right outside your door at the motel, so much the better. Remove anything of value from seats, floor, dashboard and rear window ledge. Lock the car with everything you've got. Take *all* your car keys, including duplicates, trunk keys, alarm keys and keys for extra locks, into your room with you.

10. When returning to your car after having been ʼbliged

to leave it in a less than totally satisfactory parking place, approach it with senses alert and key in hand (and heart in mouth!). Have a fast look inside before entering to make sure that no one is crouching on the rear floor. This is especially important at night. When the dome light assures you that all is well within, get in quickly, lock up, and drive off.

11. Check gas, oil, tires and so on regularly while traveling. Keep a full gas tank, and keep track of tire pressure and condition. You don't want to have the car let you down when you need her most.

Hotels and Motels

You like to think, and you probably do think, that you are safe in your hotel or motel room. Maybe you are. Some hotels are very security conscious and do a fine job of looking after their guests. But, too often, owners and managers give scarcely a thought to the necessity for an adequate all-over locking system that includes high-quality security hardware on each door. Room doors are frequently supplied with little or nothing more than those flimsy springlatches that can so easily be caseknifed or shimmed. Others are more adequately equipped, but their value is considerably reduced by masterkeying. There is not a great deal that the most experienced and well-meaning innkeeper can do to prevent a dishonest guest, an unauthorized visitor or untrustworthy staff member from duplicating any single key to use on any occasion. However, since the hotelkeeper knows this better than anyone else, it seems a pity that he would expose his guests to a locking system that makes it possible for a thief to make or obtain a master key with which he may be able to enter an entire block of rooms or perhaps every room in the place.

This doesn't happen very often, but nevertheless it does happen. The keyholder, like the skilled pickman, can have a field day once he has his hands on the key of his choice; or he can make his plans with a view to hitting one particular target—the richest guest in the place.

Thieves who make their living by preying on the rich and famous while the latter are staying at a rich and famous hotel usually plot their campaigns with considerable care and make their arrangements well in advance. The newspapers, for example, announce that the glamorous and enviably wealthy Burton Whitney-Nelsons will be staying at the plushy Jacques-Pierre Plaza for the month of June. Swiftly, the thieves go to work. If they have not already planted a housekeeper, maid, room service waiter or bellhop in the Jacques-Pierre to scout it out and wait for an appropriate victim, they will do so at once. (At least, they will attempt to. It usually isn't difficult.) By the time the Burton Whitney-Nelsons or other marks arrive, the plant has gathered all manner of useful information about the hotel and staff—and has made a duplicate of the master key. It is now a simple matter for the plant to use that key himself, or turn it over to an associate. The latter, armed with information about the layout of the hotel, the work pattern of the staff, the security arrangements, and the personal habits of the intended victims, comes on the scene at the appropriate time, looking like a well-dressed, respectable visitor himself. He visits, all right; but only in the absence of the chosen targets, and to their considerable loss.

Duplicating a key is not a difficult thing to do. It is not necessary to take it off the premises and have a copy cut; an impression can easily be made right on the spot. Soft soap will do it, for one thing, though a better method is the one that employs clay, a little oil, and hot sealing wax—plus, of course, the original key. If a key has a code number printed on it, so much the better. Then it is only necessary to take a note of the number and give it to the keymaker of the team.

Other teams of thieves, similarly operating on advance newspaper information regarding the movements of the fabulously wealthy, or simply taking a chance that sooner or later some likely marks will show up at the Beverly-Biltmore or the Ritz-Americana, will move their prize pickman right into the hotel. This involves a small investment, but it can pay off bountifully. The pickman arrives with a reservation, some expensive luggage engraved with his chosen initials, good clothing, plenty of spending money, and possibly even a phony family consisting of wife and children, all very nicely dressed and well-rehearsed.

Having settled in, the pickman can look around the hotel and even the town at his leisure. He can find out about the security staff, study the keying, do some fake business outside, take the fake family shopping, have a little fun in the evenings. . . . By no means should he make his trip too hasty, although he can do his real job in about ten or fifteen minutes. No, he must be a trusted guest, a good suspicion-luller, and he must take his time. (Why not? He's probably going to cheat on the bill when he leaves, anyway.)

At such time as it suits him he will take the lock out of the door from within, take it apart, and decode it. Then he will put it back in again, neatly and nicely so that no one will ever know that it has been removed. This procedure takes him all of ten minutes. Later, in his own good time, he will make a key to fit not only that lock but all the locks on that particular masterkey system.

There is even a way, which will not be disclosed here, whereby a very skilled lockman can make a master key to a lock without even taking the lock off the door. This is a technique that a good many legitimate locksmiths don't even know about. They may not even believe that it is possible; but we can guarantee that it can and has been done.

It is undeniable that a skilled pickman can sooner or later circumvent any particular lock; but it does seem both unfortunate and unnecessary that, after decoding the lock to any masterkeyed door, he is thereupon able to enter other rooms that are keyed under the same masterkey system. Most hotel owners and managers find it difficult to see their way around masterkeying. Some members of the hotel staff—chambermaids, for instance—must be able to enter rooms with a minimum of nuisance and delay. But there are hotels that seem to have this problem solved, and maybe they are able to do it through greater efficiency and superior housekeeping methods. In some places, for example, the chambermaids are each assigned a ring of keys. Each maid's key ring holds, permanently, one key for each room to which she is assigned during a particular work period. When she comes on the job she gets her key ring from the housekeeper, and keeps the whole ring with her during the entire work period or day. At the end of the day she returns the ring to the housekeeping or managerial office. In this way, the chambermaid is only in possession of keys to the set of rooms she is supposed to service. The same can be true of any member of the staff. Each one is accountable for the keys that they hold at the time. In this way, the hotel is protected from plants in the staff and from dishonest, key-duplicating guests. A certain amount of illicit duplicating is obviously still possible, but it is severely limited. And any thief who decodes a lock will not be able to use his knowledge to get into other rooms.

Most of us, not being terribly rich, are unlikely to fall victim to the really well-planned, elaborate hotel room theft. But chance, plus an inferior locking system, may cast us in the role of mark. In view of the inadequate locks in use in a great many hotels and motels, the wise traveler, especially one who is traveling with expensive clothes or jewelry or sales samples, will take his own locks along with him. Our consultant locksmith always carries at least two.

Several lock manufacturers make travel locks, and quite effective ones. These are little portable locks that can be used to secure doors, drawers and closets in cabins, rooming houses, hotel and motel rooms and the like. Yale is the pioneer in this field, and they call their lock (not surprisingly) the Travelok. It is inexpensive—about $6—sturdy, and extremely useful. You can use it to key-lock almost any door from the inside, and some from the outside. It also fits drawers, and closets with standard doors. It won't work on those screen-type folding doors that are sometimes used on closets in motel rooms, so if you want to secure your valuables while you are out of the room you had best put them in a drawer and lock that drawer with your Travelok. Use the top drawer, incidentally, unless there are firm partitions between the drawers. Otherwise even the dumbest of thieves can simply take out the drawer above and dip into your "locked" drawer to help himself.

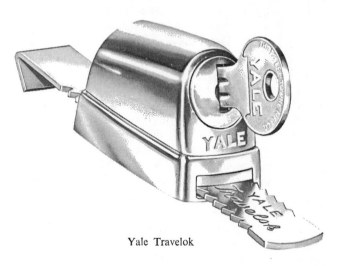

Yale Travelok

For nighttime security you can double-lock your room door simply by sliding the hooked end of the Travelok "bolt" into the lock strike, closing the door on it, pushing the holding plate against the door, and turning the key. For daytime security of your possessions, use the Travelok on that drawer or suitable closet door, and take the key with you. If by any chance your room door opens outward, you can use your second Travelok on it from the outside when you leave your room. (Don't stay out all day, though; you'll never get your room made up.)

With the keyhole type of lock, also excellent for travelers, we are treated to the spectacle of a lock locking a lock. This device is actually a keyhole filler that is made to fit the old-fashioned bit key locks still in use in the older cabins and rooming houses in the United States and quite widely used in Europe. You push it into the keyhole and snap it into locked position with its own key. When you remove the key you leave the body of the little lock in the keyhole, thus filling the keyhole with metal and effectively blocking the entrance of any other key. Only its own key will then be able to unlock your door. The Keil Lock Company makes these useful keyhole fillers, which retail for less than $2 apiece.

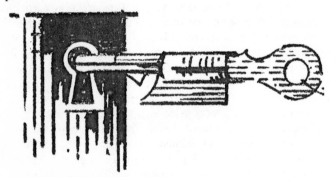

Keil Keyhole Filler

If you are the nervous type, or are obliged for any reason to hole up in a hotel or motel that you don't quite like the looks of, you might be glad of the extra protection of a little portable burglar alarm. Either the Apex or the Star, referred to in Chapter Nine, or something similar, would be suitable. You simply hang it up over or near the door and fit the springloaded clip between door and frame. Any surreptitious opening of the door will cause the clip to spring shut, make contact, and set off the alarm. If you feel that your door is sufficiently secured by your Travelok, you can use your alarm on the window.

People who travel a lot have learned not to scorn these precautions. Some—even people who really ought to have known better in the first place—have learned the hard way.

Once upon a recent time, for instance, there was a locksmith (not Schillizzi) who was attending a locksmith's convention in a major U.S. city and staying in quite a nice hotel. One evening, returning to his room after the day's meeting, he locked his room door with the standard hotel lock, put his wallet on the bedside table, undressed, and took his shower. He came out, dressed and discovered that $500 had been taken from his wallet. No travelers' checks! No Travelok! No alarm! Tch!

Meanwhile, Back Home

It is quite possible that, in spite of all the safety measures you put into effect before leaving home, some skilled thief or desperate addict may have succeeded in breaking in.

Use a little care, therefore, when you pull up in front of your home. Try to arrive in daylight. Greet your neighbors if they happen to be around, chat with them, find out how things have been. Look over your house before you go in. Case it, in effect. Don't make a big production out of it; just have a casual look around. If you see that one of your windows has been broken, or a door forced, do not go in There may be an intruder inside. Chances are he will have left, but he may still be there. Call the police at once from a neighbor's house or the nearest callbox.

If there is no sign of outside damage, enter your home in the normal way . . . except that, in this case, it's best not to rely on the principle of women and children first. A quick look around will soon tell you if the place has been entered in your absence. If there is any evidence of disarrangement, such as drawers pulled out, things scattered about, and the like, go no further. Get out quickly an dquietly, and call the police. Stay out until they arrive. Again, the intruder may still be there, or not very far away.

Should you be unfortunate enough to walk in while your place is in the process of being ransacked, or if you hear someone moving around in any part of the house, leave even more quickly than suggested above. Do not make any attempt to deal with the intruder yourself. It is perfectly true that most burglars or housebreakers prefer not to tangle with the occupant and will make every attempt to get out through some other exit when they hear you coming in, but this is not true of all intruders. You might encounter a man who is unbalanced and just as happy to attack a person as make off with property. Or perhaps there is no other exit than the one that you are blocking. You cannot be sure what the man's reaction is going to be. He may be just as scared as you are, but he is bound to be more desperate. Do *not* try to prevent him from making a rapid exit. *Do* try to make one yourself. Leave with the utmost speed. If you are lucky enough to become aware of him without him becoming aware of you, go quietly. If he does see you, yell your lungs out as you go. Screech to the neighbors to call the police, or make for the nearest telephone (not your own) yourself.

No doubt much of what has been said about self-protection and the protection of property will strike some readers as exaggerated. All those locks and bolts and bars and sirens? Such extreme caution to enter our own homes, operate our own automobiles, mind our own business? Must we really jail ourselves in our homes, our apartments, and even in our hotel rooms? Shame? What are we, a nation of neurotics?

Well. . . . A nation of thieves, maybe. But whatever we call ourselves, national crime statistics show that it is difficult to be over-cautious. Many of us may be fortunate enough to go through life without once being burglarized, or without once having to report the theft of an automobile. But luck must be guarded as carefully as anything else. If we don't look after it, we won't have it forever. All of us—every householder, every businessman, every career girl, every car owner, every traveler—must make sure of our continued good luck by protecting it with every security measure we can reasonably take. Spending a little money and taking some simple precautions are small investments against heartbreaking loss.

And when you come right down to it, it isn't *that* much for any of us to do. Things have been worse.